SOUL, SAND & SKY

SOUL, SAND & SKY

Stories and Poems of the Great Outdoors

Contents

Souls, Sand & Sky

Stories and Poems of the Great Outdoors

Copyright © 2021 The Writers' Cache

Print ISBN: 978-1-7360125-2-9

Front cover image copyright Duet PandG via Shutterstock

Back cover image copyright Tobin Akehurst via Shutterstock

Cover design copyright The Writers' Cache

✹ Created with Vellum

*For all those who venture outdoors
and return home changed*

Foreward: Going Home

E.B. Wheeler

THE "UNPRECEDENTED TIMES" of 2020 offered varied lessons to the world, but for many of us, it was a reminder of the power of the outdoors. When I let my kids play hooky from the stress and drudgery of quarantine-school-at-home for a visit to a local reservoir, I felt like I was escaping from a dark fog. The kids splashed in the chilly water and built lopsided castles from the gritty, gray sand while the seagulls screeched overhead, and the sunshine and damp breeze cleansed away the strain that had been building in my chest day by day. Everything in our human sphere was new and uncertain, but out there, the sun shone, gulls circled, and lapping waters promised peace.

With indoor venues closed in 2020, record numbers of people headed outside. Whether they sought stimulation or solace, they likely found it, rediscovering a primal need for nature, a home for the soul. For me, this reconnection took the form of a search for sand. Specifically, the colored sand caves of southern Utah, only vaguely remembered from my childhood.

My grandparents, natives of Kanab and Fredonia on the

Utah-Arizona border who had relocated to California, had a collection of bottles filled with layers of different colored southern Utah sand to remind them of home. I spent many childhood summers visiting the old family house in Kanab, playing at Lake Powell, and sometimes driving for what felt like forever (and therefore could have been ten minutes or two hours) to sandstone caves striped in hues of orange, white, purple, and even green to scrape the walls and collect own own bottles of layered sand—miniature models of the southern Utah caves and cliffs to carry with us.

Members of my grandparents' generation had scattered from their southern Utah homeland, and they eventually sold the old family home. It has since been bulldozed for new development, leaving the family plot in the Kanab cemetery as our only tangible connection to past generations in the area. But I wanted my children to experience the wonder of a wall of colors, the cool scent of damp sand, and to connect them to my past and the generations that came before them. My children had the opportunity to meet three of my four grandparents, but now all of that generation is gone. Therefore, I asked my dad where we had collected the sand so I could take my kids there.

He didn't remember.

Our parents are a link to our past. What happens when time makes those links rusty? And the pandemic threatened the older generations especially, the potential for a sudden erasure of memory and legacy. Were it not for the jars of sand, I would have nothing to prove my recollections of the sand caves were even real. My sense of urgency to find those caves increased to near-panic level.

Dad thought maybe the caves were by Coral Pink Sand Dunes State Park, massive dunes of orange-pink sand sculpted by centuries of wind into tall, shifting peaks. Recalling our forays into southern Utah, I also suspected the old Pahreah (rhymes with "Maria") ghost town might be the right location. Armed with masks and hand sanitizer, I shepherded my husband and children to one of the Kanab hotels still open during the pandemic (no breakfast, no pool, no regular cleaning service).

We tried Coral Pink Sand Dunes first. The kids brought sleds to glide down the massive hills of orange-pink sand. Even in the spring, though, the sand is hot and sucks your feet in with every step, filling shoes and socks with a fine powder that would coat our nostrils, our scalps, and the car inside and out. Regular sleds don't slip well on the hills, either, leaving the kids hot, tired, dirty, and disappointed. And, as far as we could discover, there were no colored sand caves anywhere in the area. It was, the children informed me, the worst vacation ever.

The striped hills of Pahreah looked more promising. We took our empty jars and headed into the Grand Staircase-Escalante National Monument. Along the way, we rock-hounded on BLM land for bits of jasper and petrified wood. The rough, steep roads made for some exciting ups and downs with stomach-turning views of sheer drop-offs. The few remnants of the Pahreah ghost town were interesting, and the kids had a blast climbing the colorful sandstone hills. We collected shades of sand from the hillside and observed jackrabbits and lizards darting among the sagebrush. The caves could be out there somewhere, but we didn't find them.

Returning to our home in northern Utah, I felt an overwhelming sense of failure. My children would not know the same splendid experiences that I had. The caves remained lost, and with them, a connection to the past. (I still plan to look for them, but it has become a quixotic quest.)

My brother suggests that the caves have collapsed, the walls scraped away until they could not stand. Maybe they have. The world I knew will not be the same one my children see. The changes brought by 2020 were abrupt, the slash of a ruptured fault line across the familiar landscape of our daily routines, but the scenes of my childhood have been eroding each year, the forces of technology, financial upheavals, and social revolution sculpting new vistas for my children to explore as surely as wind and water might. As the Greek philosopher Heraclitus said, "A man cannot step in the same river twice, for it is not the same river, and he is not the same man."

But I have a new bottle of sand displayed in my curio—the curio I inherited from my grandmother. The colors don't have as much variety as the older bottles, but they are vibrant, and each time I see it, I remember my children's expressions of triumph as they conquered the sandstone hills of Pahreah. Alongside the sand, we have added chunks of jasper and petrified wood collected from the red-orange landscape. And any time my husband and I want to tease our kids, we threaten another family trip to Coral Pink Sand Dunes. They shriek and laugh and beg us to go anywhere else. They made new connections to the place my family has called home for generations.

The land changes, and it changes us. I think 2020 has taught us that what John Muir said over a century ago still holds true today:

"The tendency nowadays to wander in the wilderness is delightful to see. Thousands of tired, nerve-shaken, over-civilized people are beginning to find out that going to the mountains is going home; that wilderness is a necessity; and that mountain parks and reservations are useful not only as fountains of timber and irrigating rivers, but as fountains of life. Awakening from the stupefying effects of the vice of over-industry and the deadly apathy of luxury, they are trying as best they can to mix and enrich their own little ongoings with those of Nature, and to get rid of rust and disease. Briskly venturing and roaming, some are washing off sins and cobweb cares of the devil's spinning in all-day storms on mountains; sauntering in rosiny pinewoods or in gentian meadows, brushing through chaparral, bending down and parting sweet, flowery sprays; tracing rivers to their sources, getting in touch with the nerves of Mother Earth; jumping from rock to rock, feeling the life of them, learning the songs of them, panting in the whole-souled exercise, and rejoicing in the deep, long-drawn breaths of pure wildness. This is fine and natural and full of promise... and may well be regarded as a hopeful sign of our times."

The Arrowhead Maker

Chadd VanZanten

IN THE AUTUMN of my eighth year, my father brought my older brother Marshall and me to Oak Creek Canyon in the mountains of Arizona for what would become the only family secret to which I was ever a party.

It began with a promise Dad had repeated many times. He said that when my brother and I were old enough to look after ourselves, he'd take us on our first camping trip without Mom.

"We'll head into the high country," he'd say. "Just us men."

I'm not sure why leaving our mom behind was so eagerly anticipated, but when Dad finally announced the plan one night after dinner, Marshall and I pumped our fists and cheered. My mother responded by standing up from the kitchen table and fetching a stick of chewing gum from the candy drawer. It was a habit she'd acquired to replace cigarettes. She wadded the tiny foil wrapper into a ball and pitched it into the trash, then leaned on the kitchen counter, lanky arms folded across her middle.

"What," said Dad. "What's the matter?"

"I'm still not sure about it," said Mom, pulverizing the gum with her molars. "Going so far away, just you and them."

"It's not that far," said Dad, his Adam's apple bobbing.

My father could work a slide-rule and protractor like a bespectacled wizard, but he wasn't broad-shouldered like his brother Kurt, who'd just got back from Vietnam, nor was he gritty and resourceful like Grandpa Doug, a retired forest ranger from Oregon.

Mom popped her chewing gum and examined Dad as one would an old lamp at a yard sale. His bony arms, sunken chest. Dad absorbed the scrutiny by remaining motionless, palms flat on the table, eyes darting between Mom and his half-eaten Salisbury steak.

After a long moment, Mom asked, "Why not take Uncle Kurt with you? What if someone gets hurt?"

Dad shrugged. "There's a hospital right there in Flagstaff. Can't be more than an hour from where we'll be at."

This, of course, was practically a signed admission that one or more of us would end up maimed—or worse. Mom popped her gum again. Then she turned and left the kitchen.

On the Friday before Columbus Day, our Ford station wagon was heavy laden considering the trip was just for one long weekend. Dad compensated for his lack of adventuring experience by packing for every possible contingency. There were extra sleeping bags, an entire spare tent, rope, tarpaulins, a case of pork and beans, and every lantern and flashlight to be found in our house. We had at least ten rolls of toilet paper.

"Charmin," Dad kept saying. "The good stuff."

To this matériel my mother added winter coats, rain jackets, galoshes, an umbrella, and the collective contents of our sock and underwear drawers.

Dad had taken to wearing a pair of sunglasses with big

plastic black frames and green lenses, which made him look uncharacteristically dashing. The sleeves of his heavy flannel shirt, rolled up above his elbows, gave the impression that his arms and torso were somewhat muscular.

Leaning against the garage and sucking a tiny lollipop, Mom watched with one eyebrow raised as Dad tightened up the rope on the luggage rack. Just before we embarked, Dad stepped up to her, placed a hand on the small of her back, and pulled her in close.

With her nose almost touching his, Mom pulled the lollipop from her mouth and said, "You know I never did agree to this."

Dad planted a long, deep kiss on her mouth, something I'd witnessed only a handful of times. She accepted the kiss and even kissed him back—an even rarer occurrence.

But when he turned her loose Mom said, "I still don't see why you have to go all the way up there. There's a KOA ten minutes away." With the lollipop she gestured toward town. "They have a swimming pool and a diner. And pay phones."

Dad returned to the luggage rack and fussed with the rope. "Just something I gotta do, I guess," he said.

When the station wagon was packed, which is to say there was no room remaining inside it, Marshall and I kissed our mom goodbye and, although there are details of the trip I have forgotten, I remember she cried.

"I did no such thing," she later insisted, with an extravagant eye-roll. "What's the worst that could've happened? Someone drops a hotdog in the dirt?"

But she never did hear the entire story. She never heard about Ernst and Harriet. I never told her about the arrowhead maker.

With the rear fenders riding low over the tires, we struck north through the tiny, lowland town of Sedona and into the cool high country like a well-equipped but guileless detachment of conquistadors. Ponderosa pine and juniper stood darkly green against the reddish canyon walls, while cottonwood and sycamore nestled low in the streambed, their leaves shimmering like sequins in the breeze.

Dad was an engineer for the Federal Highway Administration, and as we drove he explained how roads were constructed in such rugged country.

"It's all cuts and fills, see," he said, pointing. "They dig through this hillside to make room for the road, then they use the dug-out material to fill in a ravine someplace else. No wasted effort. Isn't that something?"

Goblinhead formations of red rock loomed along the rim of the canyon above, and their mystic stone faces seem to turn away in disapproval as we wound through the turns and curves.

Dad told us Oak Creek was a small mountain stream that even young kids could safely ford. At that time of year, however, it was red and swollen with monsoon rains. We heard the rumble and hiss of it as we drove.

"Bleedin' Jupiter," Dad exclaimed, craning his neck to glance down the gorge. "That water's high."

That afternoon we pitched our tent in a nearly empty campground within walking distance of the stream. After unpacking a few necessities, we went down to the bank to investigate. The water roared over the smooth boulders and crashed through the bends. The bloated pools boiled like great bowls of broth.

Dad stood with his arms crossed at the water's edge. "Well, the fishing's all blown out, boys," he said, gesturing dismissively at the stream. "Sorry about that. Guess that's why there's no one here."

Marshall picked up a smooth, flat stone and winged it out

into the water. Then he picked up another, but he lost his footing on the steepness of the wet clay bank. He pinwheeled his arms and nearly slid on his heels into the water, but Dad caught him by the shirt collar and pulled him back.

"Careful, Marsh. Jeeze," said Dad. "Fall in there and you'll end up in Mexico."

We didn't bother to unpack the tacklebox or any fishing rods. Instead, dad built a fire, which is to say he piled together some damp deadfall and tried in vain for thirty minutes to set it on fire by using balled-up newspaper for tinder. Of the few outdoor skills Dad possessed, his powers were weakest in the field of lighting fires. Marshall and I knew very well he'd eventually fetch a big can of lighter fluid to finish the job, but for some reason he had to try like hell without it first.

Marshall and I had seen this ritual many times. First Dad crouched at the fire pit, leaning in and blowing on the meager flames until he got lightheaded. Then he fanned the embers with a paper plate, but the dim reddish flames flickered for only a few seconds before vanishing into curls of cool gray smoke.

"I swear to god," he muttered through clenched teeth, "if I dropped a cigarette in that river over there, it'd find a way to burn this whole damn forest to the ground, but it takes twenty-five Sunday newspapers and a goddam jumbo box of matches to cook three frankfurters." The oaths and blasphemy were likewise part of Dad's firestarting ritual and did little to perturb us.

When the sun dropped beneath the canyon wall, a chill settled in around us, which Dad evidently took as the signal to begin the ritual's final stage. He stormed off, dug the lighter fluid from somewhere inside the car, and dispensed half the can onto the heap of branches and newspaper. Then he issued the requisite warning of "stand back, you kids," and tossed a burning match on top. At last there came the satisfying *woof* of ignition and the orange and blue fireball that roiled up against the dusk. Marshall and I, having whittled sharp sticks during the wait, almost immediately tilted our skewered hot dogs down over the flames.

Soon it was dark, and Marshall and I slouched and nodded in our lawn chairs. Crickets droned in the blackness, as if explaining that somewhere beyond the glow of the campfire something lurked—something that Dad had still to vanquish.

"Tomorrow," said Dad, laying on more firewood, "we'll take some sandwiches and hike up to the ghost mine."

"Ghosts?" said Marshall.

He and I traded a quick glance. It was probably unwise to use that word on us while separated from our mother in such a dark place, but Dad raised a soot-smudged hand to reassure us.

"It's just an abandoned silver mine up on the hill, Marsh. Some old buildings. I used to go up there with Grandpa Doug and Uncle Kurt. One time I found an old lantern."

Dad changed the subject by remarking on how different the night sky looked now that we were well away from the yellow glare of city lights. We gawked up at the stars, spread like a phosphorescent dust across the black velvet of space. Later on it grew cold enough that our breath smoked, and so we crawled yawning into the tent.

It rained a little that night, and in the morning the air was filled with the wet acrid smell of October. Dad squeezed the remainder of the lighter fluid onto a new pile of wood—*woof*—and cooked up a breakfast of ham and eggs in a rusty old iron skillet. There was enough left over to make six or seven sandwiches for lunch. We loaded these into an army rucksack along with some apples and then set out for the ghost mine by way of a trail that ran along the roaring stream.

Dad had not visited the place in many years, and so there

was quite a bit of head-scratching and a few wrong turns, but eventually we left the river and followed a steep trail into the trees and to the top of a great ravine, which commanded a view of several miles of canyon and the frothy stream below. Even from that height we could hear the water.

Among the juniper trees and unchecked undergrowth, there lurked tumbledown shacks and enigmatic iron frameworks. We found the remnants of an immense brick chimney. Dad kicked at the ground and unearthed fragments of glass bottles and ceramic crockery. I found a horseshoe disfigured by tumors of rust.

Dad showed us the probable layout of the abandoned compound and explained how the miners diverted water from far upstream, pressurizing it by sending it through smaller and smaller pipes.

"The pipe came down on that scaffold there, see, and when the water got to the nozzle it was blasting like a firehose. They shot it at that hillside and the slurry flowed down here, see, into troughs, you know, like big wooden bathtubs. That's how they settled out the ore. Really something, innit?"

Without Mom around, we had no one to tell us when to start and stop eating, so we explored until we were faint with hunger and then ate all the sandwiches and apples. This induced profuse flatulence, and we tried without agreement to judge whose was most sulfuric.

In the afternoon, the air grew hot and still. We gathered on the floor of a roofless, sun-bleached barracks house and before long we fell asleep to the unceasing white noise of the stream.

We awoke to the rippling peal of thunder. It rolled down the canyon and the three of us started awake at once. Without speaking, we gathered our things to head back to camp. It began to rain and the trail turned slippery. Dad was not athletic nor even very well-coordinated, and he slipped and fell more than Marshall or I. Before we were halfway down the ravine, the trail itself was crossed with numerous rivulets. We'd left behind the rain jackets and galoshes that Mom had packed for us, and so we were wet to the skin and muddy.

The last mile of trail ran along the stream, and the water rose seemingly before our eyes.

"Flash flood," Dad announced. "Let's hurry."

Entire willow trees tumbled by in the current, and the upwelling water reminded me of foamy red milk. The water had risen to the edge of the trail and in a few places the trail was under water. Dad worked hard to seem only somewhat concerned, but he had to raise his voice to be heard above the water, and that alone unnerved us.

"Know what we'll do?" he hollered over his shoulder. "We'll pack up and head down to the Indian ruins. They have cabins shaped like teepees—stay with me, boys, be careful—and there's this old guy who makes arrowheads outta flint."

He turned his head and grinned at us desperately. Marshall and I said nothing.

Dad shouted, "Won't that be something?"

From up ahead a woman came lurching up the trail toward us, flailing her arms and shrieking. I judged her to be younger than my grandmother but older than my mother, and although she wore a yellow rain slicker, her hair and clothes were soaked and splotched with mud.

Dad intercepted her, but before he could ask what the matter was, the woman clutched his sleeve and dragged him down the trail the way she'd come. Marshall and I ran after them.

As we came around a wide turn in the trail, we saw the trouble. A man had fallen into a churning bend-pool thirty feet across. He was large and muscular, but he was pinned to the massive outfall like an insect against a bathtub drain. The man wore a yellow slicker like that of the woman, and he was of the same age. He could neither free himself nor float further down, and when the water surged it covered his head.

The stream was ten or twelve feet lower than the trail in that place, at the foot of an undercut bank. The woman began to clamber down the roots and boulders. She screamed and waved hysterically at the man, but Dad grabbed her by the hood of the rain slicker and yanked her up onto the trail again. Marshall and I backed away as he shouted into her face and made her stay put. She pawed at him and jabbered on.

My father waved us over. Rain streamed down his face. In his eyes I could plainly read his fear, but there was something else, too, a comforting expression that I could not account for until years later.

He pointed to the woman and shouted, "You two stay with her."

I wasn't sure if we were to keep her away from the water or the other way round, but we went to the woman and she hugged us closely and awkwardly as she crouched in the mud sobbing.

My father backed away from the bank, and my stomach heaved as I realized he meant to jump in. He pressed his back into the underbrush like a luchador leaning on the ropes of a boxing ring. Then he ran across the trail, hurled himself from the overhanging bank, and disappeared into the water with a splash that seemed too small for all the significance it bore.

In the elongated moment before Dad surfaced, Marshall and I tore ourselves away from the woman. She snagged me

back and held me in place, but Marshall was bigger and stronger
—he got away and began to climb down to the water.

In the pool, my father sidestroked furiously to gain the far
side, then lifted himself onto the bank and knelt panting and
dripping on the rocks. His shirt clung to his back, showing the
contours of each rib and sinew. He'd lost his eyeglasses and he
was also missing one shoe, but from that side of the stream he
was almost within reach of the outfall.

The man in the yellow slicker had all but stopped struggling
against the torrent. One side of his face was in the water and his
arms trailed in the current like the branches of a waterlogged
sapling.

To reach him, my father lay flat on his stomach atop a
boulder and stretched out over the racing water. He got hold of
the man's yellow slicker, but prone as he was, he could develop
only a little leverage, so he wrenched the man inch by inch with
only the strength of his stringy arms. A few times he almost fell
in, too. However, the jostling somewhat revived the man, which
encouraged my father, and with one great lunge he pulled the
man free of the crushing flow. Then, with my father's help, the
man clawed his way onto the rocky bank, where he collapsed
gasping like some primordial amphibian.

That's when Dad spotted Marshall, who in his panic had
waded up to his hips into the water. He bawled with arms
outstretched like a toddler, stumbling. Dad begged him to move
back, but Marshall was swept into the swirling pool, where he
spun a few times like a sock in a vast washing machine before
being sucked into the outfall and immobilized against the
boulders.

I freed myself from the woman and clambered down the
bank, barking my shins and elbows on the rocks and gnarled
roots. Dad screamed at me to stop, and I did. Then he laid

himself flat again and got hold of Marshall's arm but was unable to budge him. Marshall's head was now beneath the water.

I stood at the riverbank, bleating like some lost baby animal as my father fought the water with ever-diminishing strength. Through the red-stained froth, Marshall looked very small and pale and he was not moving at all.

Then I saw the man in the yellow slicker. He had found his feet and he rose up on the bank, dwarfing my father. His long mustaches were still wet and he looked very much like a walrus. After an urgent series of shouts and gestures, the man held onto Dad's belt, which gave him greater reach, and with their combined strength they hauled Marshall to safety.

The swollen stream rumbled in its course as the rain persisted.

The nearest bridge across the stream had been swept away, and nearly an hour passed as Dad, Marshall, and the rescued man walked downstream to the next bridge to re-cross the water. Once reunited, we all embraced in a single, sodden cluster. When the couple discovered we were campers, the man, whose name was Ernst, said we must stay under a roof that night.

"Oh, that's very kind," Dad demurred, "but we've got a big cabin tent and a tarp and pork and beans and we'll be fine."

"No, young man," said Ernst, holding up a finger. "I insist and I won't take no for an answer."

My father looked at Marshall and me, wet and shivering in the rain. Then he nodded and the two men shook hands. And so that day I learned something of the ways and means of gentlemen.

We drove down the canyon to a cottage in Sedona, where Marshall and I were pampered by the woman, whose name was Harriet. We took hot baths, ate hamburgers, and guzzled at least one gallon of hot cocoa while Dad and Ernst sipped whiskey from heavy glass tumblers. When it was late, Harriet showed the three of us to a room with one large, high bed. Dad threw back the quilt and Marshall and I climbed in on either side of him.

When we had settled, Marshall asked, "Why'd you do that?"

"Do what? Help Ernst? He was in trouble."

"Would he've died?"

"Probably. Yes."

"What if you died?"

"I didn't die."

"But what if you did? And what if I would've? What then?"

"Well. That's a good question, Marsh. First of all, you had no business getting in the water that way. You're not a very strong swimmer."

"Neither are you," said Marshall.

"That's true."

"So. Why'd you do it?"

Dad thought about it.

"It was just something I had to do, I guess," he said after what seemed a long time. And there was again a quality in his voice that I could not name. Today, I believe that was the first instant that Dad himself realized what he really had done, what had really taken place.

"We were scared," said Marshall.

"I wasn't," I said, sitting up.

"Yeah you were."

I lay back down. Yeah, I was.

"Stop it, you two. I'm sorry. I was scared, too."

"You were?"

"Oh, yeah. And imagine how Ernst and Harriet felt."

We were quiet for a while. I pressed my face into the pillow and dozed.

"Boys?"

We grunted.

"Listen," said Dad. "Wake up for a sec. We need to be careful about how we tell your mother what happened at the river."

"What do you mean?"

"I mean we can't tell your mother what happened at the river."

And we never did. The three of us rarely speak of it, and to my knowledge Mom never heard anything about it.

The next day, Ernst and Harriet took us to Montezuma's Castle, an ancient dwelling chiseled into a cliff wall by the Sinagua people. Ernst was bruised and tired and needed frequent rest stops. Dad stayed by his side while Harriet took Marshall and me by our hands and bought us Indian warbonnets and ice cream cones.

We found the arrowhead maker. His face was brown and deeply lined, and his eyes were watery. He wore a traditional costume of coarse native clothing and sat outside the souvenir shop on a stubby stool of his own making. With bits of stone and antler bone, he knapped out obsidian arrowheads, which he sold for one dollar apiece.

Marshall gave the old man a dollar bill and a few minutes later he gave Marshall an arrowhead. Marshall turned it over and the sun flashed in its black, scalloped surface. I gave the old man my dollar and he began again.

With the benign bloodthirstiness that possesses certain young boys, and always thrilled to be newly beweaponed, Marshall tested the arrowhead's sharpness with his thumb and asked, "Can this thing kill a man?"

"These arrow points are not for fighting," answered the old man without looking up.

"What're they for, then?" said Marshall.

He finished the new arrowhead and placed it in my hand. "For courage."

Ernst and Dad joined us while the old man pawed through his box for a new flake of stone to work.

"Dad, he made these for us," said Marshall, holding his arrowhead for Dad to see.

"Isn't that something?" Dad produced his wallet and stood before the old man.

The arrowhead maker raised his head and blinked up at my father. There were scrapes on Dad's chin and a cut on the bridge of his nose where his glasses had been torn away. His knuckles were scuffed and red.

Dad removed a dollar bill from his wallet and offered it.

The arrowhead maker shook his head. "You don't need one of these."

The arrowhead maker turned and accepted a dollar from a girl and her father who'd just then approached. My dad stood there blinking, the unaccepted bill in his hand.

In time I would understand the look my father gave me before he jumped into the seething cauldron. It was certainty. When my father saw Ernst in the grip of the outfall, he knew his life had been reduced to a single calling and objective that would not be repudiated. Maybe he believed god wanted him to save the man. Or perhaps he viewed it as something mindless and cosmic, the endlessly complex tumblers of a lock which fell into place at random to unlock the door that opened onto his fate.

He never explained it to me, but as I recall Dad returning the dollar bill to his wallet, I know now that it didn't matter. He was not a ranger or a warrior, and he was never again called on to rise to such an act of heroism—unless you count the courage it took to refrain from telling my mother the true story when she got after him for losing his glasses. But even if Dad had not been chosen to save Ernst that day at the river, I feel that the arrowhead maker would have known to withhold his token.

Maguire Primrose

Shanan Ballam

I stop at the secret place in the canyon
where only a few know where to find them
and wade through scraping brush and branches
with binoculars, past the sprawling willow, ascend

the crumbling ridge. There: magenta saucers
filled with sunlight spilling out through golden
stamen dabbed with pollen. May pauses
with their beauty, their scarcity, interwoven

with my life. What more can I do to save
myself but to learn the language of flowers,
learn to glow like a fierce star, to stand brave
and erect in falling snow, withstand hours

of savage canyon wind, ripping rain, so cruel.
I survive rooted to earth, brilliant jewel.

Five Minutes

Dustin Earl

WITH THE GLIMPSE of flowering blossoms rustling in an April breeze or the orange beams of a sunset on wispy clouds, there are times when I catch a glimmer of beauty that stays with me forever. This is why I climb mountains. Only where earth meets sky, can I truly feel free, if for only five minutes.

In the summer of 2008, I arrived in Japan fresh out of college and ready to show the world what I could do. I planned to climb Mt. Fuji as a grand welcoming to the land of the rising sun. Conquering Fuji-san was like conquering myself, proof that I could endure my years away from home.

Unlike the other mountains I've climbed, Mt. Fuji rises so prominently over packed cities and mountainous landscape that it dominates the skyline for more than a hundred miles. It is the subject of countless poems, photographs and artwork, and it is the single most recognizable symbol of Japan.

The best peaks offer more than just a good view; they offer an array of life, nature, and landscape. The trail up Mt. Naomi in Northern Utah passes through meadows thick with wildflowers that slope into an alpine wilderness. Teewinot in the Wyoming Tetons is not for the faint of heart, with its steep trails and dangerous cliffs, rising to a pinnacle that drops a sheer three thousand feet into Cascade Canyon.

Mt. Fuji, an active volcano, offers rocks. Big rocks, small rocks, round rocks, sharp rocks, lots and lots of boring, brown rocks.

To be fair, I only climbed the upper part of Fuji-san. A lush landscape surrounds the lower half, but that isn't where people usually start, and like most people, I began my ascent just below tree line at the Subaru Fifth Station on the Yoshida trail, *Yoshida Subaru Gogome*.

The fifth station is a tourist trap, and with the exception of a small Shinto shrine, the hotels and shops looked like a tacky alpine village. If I didn't know any better, I'd have sworn I was in a ski resort.

Mt. Fuji itself looms over the hotels and souvenir shops, or so I imagined, were it not for the clouds blocking the view. Fuji-san is an extraordinarily shy mountain. She's so large she has her own weather patterns and gladly snatches nearby clouds to wrap around herself like a fluffy blanket.

Every good hike needs a walking stick, and with my favorites still back in the U.S., I perused the shops whose selections included a variety of staffs, each with intricately carved mountain gods or local animals. I opted for a plain, four-foot wooden pole. This has since become one of my best hiking sticks.

Two Japanese signs marked the trailhead on the far side of the fifth station, and a line of haggard returning hikers ambled past as I took my first steps onto the trail. They leaned on their own walking sticks, cringing with each step. I gulped and sped on, the path couldn't be *that* difficult, could it?

Lush trees and pink flowers lined the way, and the hum of cicada song punctuated the ambience. Miniature shrines dedicated to the mountain gods dotted the path, and one such statue stood winking at passersby with a small pile of coins at its base. I couldn't decide whether his expression wished good luck or was meant to encourage donation. I still had a few pennies in my wallet, so I left them for him, hoping that American currency would bring as much luck as Japanese.

It didn't.

The trees soon parted at the sixth station, *Rokugome*. From here, the land below stretched into the horizon, growing from a canopy of green. Sadly, all I saw was gray fog. The trail widened, zigzagging into the mists as the ascent began in earnest. Most people turned back here, satisfied with the forty-minute nature trail.

I climbed into the drifting haze above, and it dampened the sound of other hikers, leaving me isolated with my thoughts. For the first time, I contemplated what I was doing. Here I was, on the other side of the world, and climbing a mountain I'd only seen in pictures or film. The thought invigorated my muscles and drove me on. I'd worked for years to finish my degrees and move out into the world, and now at last, I was here.

There's a saying in China, "He who does not reach the Great Wall is not a true man." The Japanese have a similar phrase, *"Fuji-san, ichido mo noboranu baka, nido noboru baka."* This roughly translated as, "He who has never climbed Mt. Fuji is a fool, and he who climbs it twice is a greater fool." In China, I passed my test into manhood, and now I would prove I was no fool.

Still, what about climbing Mt. Fuji twice made you a greater fool?

The path gradually narrowed until the switchbacks stopped

at the seventh station, *Nanagome*, a collection of mountain huts offering lodging, overpriced food, and outrageously expensive water. Each hut also offered a special hot iron stamp for your walking stick as proof you'd made it this far. For a price, of course. I leaned on my pole and sighed as the man pressed an iron to my stick.

I felt like such a tourist.

Nanagome, the seventh station. The word "*nana*" in Japanese means "seven," but there's also another word for it, *shichi*. "*Shi*" has connotations with death, so while *Shichigome* means "the seventh station," in liberal interpretation, it could also mean "the death station." Not a particularly pleasant thought and I wondered why my mind focused on that obscure aspect of the Japanese vernacular.

I'd passed hundreds of people on the trail, but it was those in their sixties, seventies, and dare I say eighties that impressed me the most. They huffed, moved slowly, but kept going. Their determination reminded me of Ulrich Inderbinen, a mountain guide who scaled the Matterhorn in the Swiss Alps three-hundred and seventy times, with his last ascent being at the age of ninety. He'd continued to climb other alpine peaks until retiring at ninety-five.

The sky cleared. At last, I could see the top, closer than I'd anticipated. Both my legs and feet rejoiced. I already felt bruises on the bottom of my feet, and a blister growing under my little toe didn't help. I sat on one of the benches at *Nanagome* and eased my shoes off, spilling out the tiny stones that'd fallen in. My soles were red. It's amazing how much lava rock hurts, even through thick shoes.

Here and there, patches of green dotted the brownish slope, and an occasional bird darted about, snatching insects. A small cliff of rock jutted from the top and was the only feature of note. When compared to the Idol and Worshiper on Mt. Teewinot, it wasn't much to look at. Still, that was my goal, and I would meet it before sundown.

The clouds stretched and pulled back like wispy fingers reaching for an endless sky. One in particular rose like a menacing shadow over the others, and for the first time, I began to question the wisdom of climbing the tallest mountain in Japan while a tropical storm hovered off the Honshu coast.

Fuji-san's shadow reached over the clouds in a perfect cone. It grew, moving like a stalker through the mists as the hours waned.

The higher I climbed, the more difficult it became to breathe, with each inhale harder than the last. My muscles tingled and my head spun with the beginnings of altitude sickness. Although sleeping in the huts at the top would help me acclimatize, this was going to be a long, headache filled night.

A sinking pit welled in my stomach as I neared the rocky outcropping. There were ten stations, and if I was near the top, why hadn't I come across the eighth yet?

I sighed. Yes, this "top" was the eighth station, *Hachigome*. I looked back at the rocky outcropping I wrongly thought my goal. It now sat at least two or three hundred feet below.

The sky brightened with the last shades of twilight and when the slivers of pinkish sunlight faded, the moon rose like a pale lantern, illuminating distant clouds.

I looked for the altitude marker and my heart sank. I still had more than four hundred and thirty-six meters to go! Fourteen hundred feet! It was like climbing every step in the Empire State Building with another four hundred left to spare.

The man in the last hut looked with trepidation at the path ahead, and advised me to stay there for the night since I hadn't brought a flashlight. I looked up, this time not at a false top, but the real goal. I shook my head. No. I set out to climb this mountain today, and I was going to do it. I came to Japan for the experience, and if I stopped now I might as well turn around and go home. I needed to prove I could do it. If I succeeded, then perhaps I could find a place in the land of the rising sun. I held out my staff and paid the man to stamp it, proof that I'd at least made it this far. He sighed and gave me a knowing look, as if I'd not been the first to ignore his sound advice.

I trudged on, stubborn determination carrying my steps far above *Hachigome*. I looked back at the line of headlamps and flashlights dotting the trail between the seventh and eighth stations. None followed past that point.

I was alone on the mountain, just like I was alone in Japan.

The clouds crept back so slowly that I didn't notice until they'd completely obscured the moon, leaving me in darkness. The rising winds chilled my skin and the last leg of the journey sapped my stamina. At this height, the lack of oxygen makes each step an expression of sheer will. Altitude sickness is a little like having the flu; your skin tingles and all of your muscles lose their strength.

To keep myself going, I counted my steps. One. Two. Three. Every time I reached fifty, I'd stop to catch my breath. Again. One. Two. Three. Ten. Twenty. Or was that Twenty-one? My oxygen-deprived mind lost itself in the simplicities of basic math.

The ninth station, *Kyugome*, was little more than a trail marker. No hot food, no warming huts, and no one to stamp my stick. More rocks had collected inside of my shoes and the blister on my toe was now the throbbing size of my thumbnail. My will to go on faded and I looked back at the "death station" far below and struggled to banish unpleasant thoughts of my own demise.

Then the rain started.

Water pelted my face in gusts that blew me about while I felt my way up the trail with my walking stick. The mountain winds howled, and shivering, I drew my jacket around my neck.

What was I doing? Why was I here? Not just on Mt. Fuji, but in Japan? I stood on the opposite side of the world, with an ocean between me and my home. I wanted independence, freedom, but I was fresh out of college. It was like I'd jumped into the deep end of the pool without checking whether I could swim.

One. Two. Three. The winds whisked my words away. Aching, soaked and chilled I rounded a bend and squinted to see a torii gate. *Jugome.* The last station! Only two more switchbacks stood between me and a warm blanket. My knees buckled under the pressure, but gasping for breath, I carried myself up and passed through the threshold.

I looked about. Why was it dark?

I walked past the mountain shacks in confused bewilderment. I'd taken too long to get here and they'd closed for the night.

Years ago, during a particularly cold day in Switzerland I got caught in *die Bieza,* a bone-chilling winter wind common in the alpine valleys. I experienced a case of mild hypothermia where my core body temperature dropped several degrees. I spend an hour in a warm bath, but it wasn't until about a week later when my body completely recovered.

My frantic knocks on the doors went unheeded, and I brought my knees to my chest as I shivered and slumped against one of the buildings to huddle out of the storm. The air prickled my skin and blew almost as cold as it had in Switzerland, only this time with a chill rain. I'd conquered the summit of Mt. Fuji, but she wouldn't yield a victory so easily. Was this what it was like actually living out in the world, away from a sheltered college life? I was woefully unprepared for this mountain, so was I likewise unprepared to live away from home?

A group of people from India who'd also braved the hike arrived thirty minutes later, and we kept each other company until someone noticed us and opened the door.

The warm perfume of kerosene rushed into my face as I stepped into the hut. My wet clothes clung to my skin, and after paying the mandatory fee, I took my bed, bunked among dozens of others. The heavy blankets soothed my muscles and I drifted into restless sleep.

I woke to the commotion of hundreds of people. Stumbling from my bunk, tired and stiff, my clothes still wet, I glanced through the crowd. Many had spent the night, but many more had climbed after the rains had died down earlier that morning. Everywhere people slurped small bowls of soba noodles and drank green tea.

I stepped outside and scowled. Clouds had covered the mountain again, obscuring any view of the legendary Fuji sunrise.

I walked the caldera, up above the *Jugome* and away from the crowds. I wanted to be alone when the sun rose, even if I couldn't see it. I stared at the reddening glow, disappointed. All of that effort and no sunrise. Worse yet, the hike back down would probably be nothing but a dull, gray fog.

As if in answer to my disheartened inner voice, or in reward for coming this far, Fuji-san showed compassion, and she parted the vapor.

Below, the clouds rolled in a sea of violet, and above, they coalesced into a ceiling of wavy red. The sky between opened into a narrow corridor that stretched into a horizon of shimmering gold.

Rising like a red orb, the sun peeked over the blanket like a shy child gauging an audience. From the station below, people called to it, raising their hands three times and cheering in unison. *"Banzai! Banzai! Banzai!"*

For five minutes I stared awestruck at the halo of color. For five minutes I was free. Free of care, worry, or pain. My cramped legs became a distant moan, and my headache faded into the first light of the rising sun.

Fuji-san gave me a moment of paradise that I'll ever thank her for. The fog soon rushed across the caldera, again obscuring the horizon and leaving me with a bright, gray haze.

It was enough.

One of the men at the tenth station, *Jugome*, stamped my stick with bright red *kanji*, Japanese characters proving that I'd made it. That stick sits in the corner of my room, and every time I look at it, that red mark serves as a reminder of Fuji-san, and the lessons she taught.

I climb mountains for those rare moments when, in the freedom offered by the high places of the world, I catch a glimpse of beauty and understand what it means to live. Though an ocean stood between me and my home, I now knew I could face what Japan offered. As long as she, from time to time, gave me five minutes.

First published in *Volatile When Mixed.*

5

Bear Lake

Britt Allen

Your heart could bleed out
on the suddenness of all that blue,
sharp aqua lake laid
in a nest of rabbitbrush and sage.

Into the blue, five sisters swam
past their hips, breasts, and necks
swam to their nostrils and tip-toes
tugging a single shared inflatable chair.

Every woman is weightless in water:
not homeless, not hungover,
not married, not divorced,
not children, not mothers,

all bodies dissolving,
their surnames left on shore
with the flip-flops and wedding rings.

6

Rambina

E.B. Wheeler

I'm not fond of sleeping on the ground or peeing in the woods, but they come with the territory when backpacking, and backpacking is for people who are tough. People who are confident. People who have it all together.

After high school, I was none of those things. The financial aid for my college of choice fell through at the last minute. As my high school friends pursued their higher educations at prestigious schools across California, I was treading water. It was perhaps the most frightening thing that had happened in my eighteen years, finding myself in a stare-down with the adult world, where good grades and your circle of friends don't solve all your problems.

One day, I came home from classes at the local second-rate junior college to find my dad and teenage brothers leaning over a map on the dining room table.

"What are you doing?" I asked.

"We're planning a trip—backpacking in the San Bernardinos with the Larsons."

Many people picture Southern California as one giant, sprawling mega city filled with Hollywood stars and gang members. But the San Bernardino Mountains stretch above the traffic and pollution, pushed upwards by the San Andreas fault and teeming with the mountain lions and bears that make occasional appearances in the asphalt-coated wilderness below. The mountains are a refuge: something wild, natural, and free, rising over the structured, man-made world.

"I want to go too," I said, surprising myself.

Our family camped fairly often, but I had been unenthusiastic since the trip where everyone got food poisoning and my youngest brother barfed in the tent, all over my head. Rinsing out my long hair in the weak KOA showers had not been pleasant. And I wasn't exactly athletic, though I rode my bike and occasionally took the dog for a run, so I figured I was in decent enough shape for backpacking.

A couple of weeks later, when we were a few hours into our hike, my feet let me know how wrong I was. Tingles of pain raced up my legs with each step. My pack, which started at about twenty pounds, now weighed at least one-hundred-twenty. I didn't dare ask how much farther we had to go, because that would pull me out of the now, and now was all I could handle. The way each breath scratched through my lungs, I was sure I was going to collapse before we made it to our campsite anyway.

Luckily for me, our family friend Todd Larson was a doctor – an ER surgeon, in fact. Tall and bulky, he lumbered along in front of me. I kept my gaze locked on his bright red pack as if the sight of it could drag me along. His teenage boy and girl raced ahead of him with my two brothers. I was caboose, but I would've rather fallen behind and let the coyotes eat me than admit I couldn't keep up. Despite my protesting feet, I pressed forward.

One step at a time, I dragged myself into the primitive campsite. The boys, all well versed in scouting, had the tents up and the fire crackling. Without much else to do, I whittled roasting sticks, a piece of mosquito net draped over my camo hat to keep the bugs from eating my face.

"Thanks," Dr. Larson said, taking one of the sticks from me. "Hey, you look like a girl version of Rambo in that outfit. Like...Rambina!"

I chuckled along with the others to cover the sting of embarrassment. Some action hero I was. My legs hurt so much I wasn't sure I could move, and I'd pretty much decided not to eat or drink the whole time to minimize nature's call. I popped a piece of mint gum in my mouth. Other than playing with my pocket knife, I was about as out of place as, well, a Southern California girl on a campout in the mountains. Casey, Dr. Larson's daughter, was just hanging around the campsite as well, but she was twelve. No one expected much from her.

We cleaned up after dinner, told some campfire stories, and headed for bed. The boys shared one tent, Casey slept in mine, and my dad and Dr. Larson camped out under the stars.

"Don't leave any food in your tents," my dad said, hoisting the pack with tomorrow's breakfast and dinner over a branch in a bear bag.

Rocks poked me through the floor of the tent, but my exhaustion lulled me into a shallow sleep.

Sometime in the deep quiet of the night, a rustle outside the tent woke me. Maybe a raccoon. Or a skunk. Yuck. What would we do if it sprayed the tent? I listened.

Branches cracked and grunted breaths pressed against the tent. No, this was something big. Really big. Wuffling around my tent. I curled deeper into my sleeping bag. Bobcat? Mountain lion? Bear?

Moving so slowly that the fabric of my sleeping bag didn't even whisper, I felt around the little backpacking tent. All I had was a pocket knife and a thin veil of nylon between myself and something large and undoubtedly hungry. There was no food in the tent, but I did have gum in my bag. Despite the cool of the night, sweat broke out over my skin. Did gum count as food? Was I going to get mauled over a pack of Trident?

Some more shuffling against the tent, and a distant male voice—my dad or Dr. Larson, too quiet for me to tell—whispered, "Bear!"

Yep, I was going to die. And what about Casey? She was still asleep. I was the adult. I had to try to protect her. Normally, my dad would have a gun, but they weren't allowed in the national forest. Of all the times to obey the rules. I grabbed my stupid little pocket knife and held it tight. Each breath of chilly air seemed to settle into a hard, icy lump in my stomach. The bear pawed at the tent. It would rip through the fabric any moment. I would jab it in the eye or the throat. Then it could eat me while Casey escaped.

The shuffling moved away. Towards the no-longer-sleeping men. Now what was I supposed to do? There was a tearing sound. No yelling. Just snuffling and ripping. People would scream if a bear was eating them, right?

The campsite grew quiet. The adrenaline pulsed out of my system, and I trembled. What was I supposed to do? Stay in the tent? See if the bear had eaten someone? There in my sleeping bag, not knowing, I could cling to the illusion of safety. But what if my dad or Dr. Larson were hurt, or the bear went after my brothers' tent? Not that I could do anything for them, but I had to find out what had happened.

The sound of my tent's zipper was like the crackle of fireworks in the stillness. I raised it slowly, one click at a time.

We'd put the fire out, so I crawled from the tent with my flashlight and examined the wreckage. Scraps of red fabric scattered around the campsite. Not bloody. Just a bright red. Dr. Larson's pack.

"I left a granola bar in it," Dr. Larson said from the darkness.

I jumped and swung my flashlight around. My dad shook his head at Dr. Larson and went to check on the bear bags. Dr. Larson lit the fire, and I helped stoke it with the branches my brothers had gathered earlier. My trembling had nearly worn off, and my cold sweat dried in the night breeze. The fire helped, answering primitive fear with a primordial feeling of power, control over nature.

I stared into the flickering light, and a shadow moved across from me. The hairs on the back of my neck pricked to attention, and I rose. The bear. The bear waited on the other side of the fire, watching me through the low flames, a huge black form like the darkness of the forest wrapped in fur. Its eyes glittered in the firelight.

Dr. Larson yelped. I knew the expression, "screamed like a girl," but had never heard it put into practice until he shrieked. Then he jumped behind me, his human shield, a good foot shorter and two hundred pounds lighter than him.

My chest constricted around my heart's crazy rhythm calling escape, escape, escape. I screamed too. But not "like a girl." Anger rushed through me—anger at the bear and at Dr. Larson and at life's frustrations and setbacks. I roared and waved my arms. More like a bear. I always assumed I fell on the "flight" end of the "fight-or-flight" spectrum, but something rose up inside of me to answer the challenge of the creature staring me down.

The bear rose up on its hind legs, and I braced myself. Would it leap over the fire or charge around? It sniffed the air then dropped down and lumbered back into the darkness.

We stood listening to the night. Crickets chirped and small creatures rustled in the undergrowth, but the bear didn't return.

I collapsed on a log next to the fire and gave Dr. Larson a withering look. "Really?"

He grinned sheepishly. "I'm a surgeon. I could have stitched you back up."

"What happened?" My dad wielded his gigantic Maglite flashlight like a club. The boys stuck their heads out of the tent.

Dr. Larson spoke before I could. "The bear came back. Rambina here scared it away."

And this time, I grinned at the nickname and basked in a flush of pride. I might not have everything together, but I could face the bears that life threw at me.

7

Beach Therapy

Alice M. Batzel

The sea calls to her
over meadow, desert, mountain,
wherever she may be.
The whisper of the breeze
carries her to water and shore,
safely at a harbor in her memory.

She sits in solitude,
watching the endless blue ocean,
sorting through what is,
reflecting on loss,
dreaming of what might have been,
imagining what still could be.

Wounds of the heart, missed opportunities,
questions of life, unmet dreams,
long for answers and peace.
Reliable rhythmic waves,

the salty air's warm embrace,
comfort and mend her brokenness.

Expansive sky and vast ocean
give her sanctuary and solace,
to safely search her soul.
Emptiness finds filling,
longing finds hope,
hurt finds healing.

Wherever she may be, the sea calls to her.
She answers with willing heart, mind, and body,
transporting her through time and space.
In meditative commune with ocean and shore,
she places her feet in the seaside water,
opens her soul...and breathes.

$$\overline{}$$

8

Where Gulls Dance

Betti Avari

$$\overline{}$$

"Come in and sit down."

I step inside, and his office smells like mint. My manager has a nervous chewing habit.

"Philip? Is everything alright?" It's a quarter to five. Rumbling engines at the construction site outside his window make his door shake on its hinges as I close it and sit down.

This is his usual behavior before assigning me a big project. Philip rubs his chin for a moment, like he's gathering his thoughts. Or maybe his courage. At last he sighs. "I know this is probably catching you off guard, but we're letting you go."

Beeping from a dump truck echoes right outside the window. I lean forward. "I'm sorry?"

"We're letting you go."

Frozen in this leaning position, I try to shake the shock from my system to process what is happening. Is this a cruel nightmare?

"What?" I feel my pulse in my lips, hear it echo through my head as I stammer, "Wh-why?"

"The firm is moving in a different direction."

I'm still trying to process, and Philip is still trying to keep his composure. Surely, he's joking, even if his expression is serious.

I'm a model employee. I embody the Boy Scout oath. Friendly, helpful...all of it.

"A different direction...than what?" I sound incredulous, I know, but I keep my voice steady and my expression neutral. "What have I done wrong?"

"You've done nothing wrong."

I realize that he has just assigned me my biggest project yet. I can't convince him, there was never a chance of that. A few flourishes of the pen, and it's over. I sign what Philip calls a letter of resignation—offered as a loophole so I don't have to admit to being fired on future job applications.

Fired?

I've never been fired before. Is this why I feel so lost? I don't know where to begin to find myself again.

Forget finding myself! My goal is to keep as much dignity as possible. I'll find myself later.

I set his pen on his shiny new glass-top desk and look up at the clock. Three minutes. That's all the time it takes to make my future plans and all of my career goals and dreams obsolete. Make *me* obsolete. This moment takes so much more from me than time. It's stolen my occupation, my identity. I even feel robbed of these one hundred and eighty seconds that it takes to close up any loose ends that aren't my future. It's time to stand up from the shiny desk where I've been let go. My knees tremble as I rise.

Philip holds his door open and offers me a cardboard box. I blink. A box for my belongings. The odor of stale mint haunts me as I walk to my desk.

My life fits in a single cardboard box: my pictures, framed

education certificates, planner, paperweight, set of pens, and reading glasses...all of it. I reach in my drawer for a piece of gum and realize with a start that I will never reach into this desk again. I stare at the open drawer. The reality and horror of the moment sinks in. I don't want the taste of mint in my mouth; the smell is cloying now. It's a reminder of my anxious manager who has offered me an empty box and an empty future; I drop the nearly-new package in the wastebasket at my feet.

My last act as an employee is to turn over the office keys. In ceremonious fashion, I remove them from my carabiner and set them on the desk as Philip steps around the corner and glances at his watch meaningfully; he wants to be home in time for dinner. I can't bring myself to look at this man who shared a casual business lunch with me yesterday without so much as a hint of what was coming today.

My gaze settles on the screensaver. A collage of my family photos has been replaced by a generic landscape with a big rock on a rosy sunset beach. The sand is washed smooth and clean, and the rock is surrounded by currents, wind and waves. Somehow, the photograph of that rock standing there strong and defiant gives me courage and fortifies my determination.

On any other day, that image would have been just another beautiful but generic vista, but today, it means something to me.

"Five o'clock already? No need for theatrics, Philip, I'm packed." I gesture to the keys. "Front door, office, and desk."

He snatches them up—as if I might try to steal them back. In return, he hands me a photocopy of my signed letter of resignation, which I slip inside my box of belongings. I fit the lid on top of the box and the next question floats to the surface: how do I walk away from this place?

The answer? One foot in front of the other.

As I walk out the doors, in my peripheral I catch Philip

bending over to retrieve my discarded pack of gum from the wastebasket.

———

"Hey," my sister reaches for her water glass and pulls me back to the present. "You okay?"

All evening, she and my spouse have flanked me.

Across the diner, someone jingles their keys. I think of my own keychain that is now three keys lighter. I sigh and lean on my sister's shoulder as I answer her question. "I don't know. But I will be. I'm still standing, right?"

I wish I could tell my sister that I'll stop worrying tonight, that I won't let myself remember that desk drawer that isn't mine anymore, because I already walked out of that office for the last time today...but what's the point of making empty promises? I'm sure I will relive those last moments frequently over the coming days.

Sitting here in this diner, I'm safe. I'm smelling apple pie, not mint. A little key jingle might trigger me today, but I'll get over it sooner or later. Still, I have to think about where the mortgage payment will come from in a few months when our savings account runs dry if I don't find a new desk to call my own.

"Still *standing*? You should be dancing," my sister says. She reminds me that I also need a bit of joy in my life, and recommends a grounding technique she learned online to manage stress. "Focus on a few things in the room. They ground you in the present moment so your worries can take a back burner."

I notice the live edge dining table, the smell of maple syrup in the air, and the sounds of laughter and bright conversation all around me. I sigh. She's right. For now I'm going to focus on my loved ones, the smiles captured in each screensaver that I deleted.

They are right here, sitting around this table. They weren't deleted, canceled, or fired. They're stored on the hard drive of my heart—they're stitched into the elements of my life—supporting me, not tearing me down, and they aren't going anywhere. They are the foundation that keeps me standing. Do they know how much it strengthens me to see my daughters laughing with my nephew, playing with the blueberries on his pancake, making a frown turn upside down?

———

I wake early. The sound of the surf penetrates the aging motel walls and rumbles in my bones. It's been a month. And a thousand miles.

I've driven for two days to reach this place on the Oregon coast. It's not far from the fresh grave of my cousin Alex, a young life cut short. After suffering an onslaught of physical storms that couldn't be withstood, his health eroded, and now he's nothing but ashes and dust. The suffering of his grieving family and young widow add to the turmoil that's been churning in my veins for the past month.

The restlessness that has built within me since I was "let go" is clawing for release. I kiss my sleeping family and leave a note on the nightstand.

Going for a walk on the beach. I'll be back by 9:00.

Every muscle used for crying is weak and shaky as I step outside and breathe in the salt air.

We arrived after dark last night. The sky, pitch black, refused to shed even a little light. I could hear the waves of the vast ocean as we unpacked, but there was only dark sky to the west of us. Now, as I take in the vista in the misty morning light, I gasp.

I stand before an expanse of waving grass on knobby dunes, a gray blue haze hovering above the waves, stretching across the sky, and a field of sand as far as the eye can see, riddled with water ponds that look like stretch marks. And here at the continent's edge, rooted among all of this grandeur, is my rock.

It's here. The lonely rock on my screensaver that bolstered me that last day of work. The behemoth rock is standing in the surf in front of *my* motel.

This is a sign. I know it is.

Frozen in the parking lot of this beachfront motel caught at a last minute bargain, I marvel at the priceless view.

My gaze scans the expanse from north to south and back to north: the distant cloud of mist, the cacophony of the waves, the noisy gulls and the dancing grass of the dunes. The stark strength of these natural elements all pay homage to the rock that has withstood countless storms.

I don't know how this rock still stands. The nearest mountain is at least two miles away. It must have been abandoned by the soft soil that surrounded it, but like the mountains in the distance, the rock stands firm.

This is my rock.

The roaring waves don't matter—the saturated job market, the interviews I've nailed without getting the callback, the unemployment meetings that were so demoralizing, learning weeks later that nepotism was to blame for my job loss—those faded moments lose their importance. Because the rock is stronger than the forces between the mountains. And so am I.

The rumbling waves echo in my chest, but I have never felt more stable, never felt more sure. I step onto the soft sand dunes of the beach. Yes, I too am a rock, and I belong.

One foot in front of another, I allow the decline and the sea to pull me in. The beach welcomes my weary soul. I feel myself sinking a little deeper into this soft surface. Yet, these steps are easier to take than others in my recent past.

The sand cradles my every step, and it doesn't ask, "Why should we hire you?" It just lifts me up where I stand.

The fresh salt air cleanses the vestiges of stale mint from my senses. The breeze coming off the water tugs at me, tests me. It pulls at my jacket and drags through my hair, but I stand firm, raise my face to the wind. I hear the gulls dancing high overhead, and I open my arms, wide. Like the gulls, I trust in my instincts and in my wings to ride the gusts of wind that carry me. Like the rock, I stand firm.

But the water invites me closer with each wave, like the beating pulse in a mother's breast. The future is inviting me to come out and dance.

My knees aren't trembling anymore. What once was an aimless stumble now has purpose. I have purpose. For the first time in a month, I know where I'm going. Down to the water. Down to the surf. Down to the massive rock. My symbol of strength.

"I'm letting you go." I whisper to the past. "And I'm moving in a different direction—my own direction."

I give up the ghost of the old life, and take on a life of self-worth that needs no validation. With a hope as tangible as the salt air in my lungs, I go down to the water and step into the foaming grandeur of living nature. The water pulls me in, welcomes me.

I take a slow, deep breath, step one foot in front of the other, slowly at first, then faster. Soon, I'm dancing among the waves. I dive in and join the froth and bracken. With each wave and each plunge, I allow the waves to carry me like driftwood. They polish and smooth my soul as my big rock towers beside me.

Wave upon wave, I am renewed and strengthened. I know how the rock gains its strength. It accepts the ebb and the flow. And so shall I.

I want to share this moment with my daughters, but they wouldn't understand.

Someday, when they're older, I'll teach them of the rise and fall of the tides in our lives and point out the anchors that hold us in place when the riptides seek to displace us. Their storms will come, and as long as I breathe, I'll be their breakwater for the strongest waves, protective and surrounding until they too can dance again.

I send a grateful word to my rock, to the waves, to the wind and the gulls in the sky—my eyes closed, my heart steady. My life doesn't fit into one little box. It expands as far as the eye can see, to the distant wave, to the distant shore. My laughter echoes in the cradles of the waves, and I am whole.

9

Drake

Star Coulbrooke

On the sidewalk
between Smithfield Implement
and the city library, a greenhead
stands vigil over his mate,
brown hen knocked to the grass
between highway and sidewalk
where the drake mourns.

What else could it be
but mourning?

What of their eggs
in the nest along Summit Creek
where they roosted next to the park
with its church repurposed
for basketball, spire taken down,
arched windows bricked over?

We wonder on the second day
if we should move her closer
to water, away from the highway,
less visible to dogs and kids.

Would we stand here,
would we, on the third day
as he does,
diminishing in weight,
his beak opening, closing
as we come to watch him
as he stands there near her?

The sun sets and dusk falls,
and he does not leave her
as we leave them
in this place of impossible grief.

10

The Weeping Willow at Goblin Creek

McKel Jensen

WE WERE the girls that looked alike. Our peers and teachers constantly asked if we were sisters, but as far as we knew, we had no relation; no common thread on a family tree, unless you count our weeping willow as family—that we could both claim.

"We're fourth cousins on my mother's side," I would lie when people asked, but the truth was, we had no idea what a fourth cousin was.

We met one afternoon after school when I decided to take a long way home in the hope of avoiding my sister's annoying friends. I stumbled upon a beautiful weeping willow off the path behind my neighborhood. Laurel was sitting under the tree reading a book. She had long, thick brown hair with her bangs braided to the side. Having just moved to Utah from California with her family, she had been out exploring and discovered the tree as a perfect reading haven.

"Hey," I said. "What an amazing hideout! Can I join you?"

"Sure, come sit down," she responded. "My name is Laurel.

Would you like a Fruit Roll-up? I have an extra." Laurel reached inside a small backpack and handed me a treat.

And that was that. We were instant friends—as if we had known each other for years.

Our willow tree, just barely out of view of suburban fences and sodded lawns, became our sanctuary. Sometimes we could hear a nearby street, and every Friday was interrupted by the buzz of a distant lawnmower, but there in that field was our wilderness: our suburban oasis.

Laurel used to laugh at the way I said things. "Why do you say 'spirit-chul' instead of 'spiritual'?" she asked.

"I don't know. That is just how I talk—that's how everyone talks," I responded, still wondering what was so weird about it.

Soon after, she asked me to say "spiritual mountain" and laughed even harder when it came out as "spirit-chul mow-un."

I will admit it was funny to see how much she enjoyed this joke. She also helped me realize that our school's name, Cottonwood, did in fact have two *t*'s in it.

From the beginning, we loved to find adventure. Behind my neighborhood ran a creek. Whenever we didn't have school, we would cut through the parking lot at the Presbyterian Church on Vine Street and climb the levee to the grassy path along the waterway we called "Goblin Creek."

"Do you think the goblins have been there?" she asked.

"What are we? Five?" I retorted, but in my heart, I believed the goblins had done their magic yet again in bringing our place to life. "I hope so," I resigned.

"Maybe we should start calling them 'hobgoblins,'" Laurel said, "I learned in Ms. Baker's Shakespeare class that goblins are the mean ones, but hobgoblins are magical."

"Right," I said, pretending to have heard the term 'hobgoblin' before. "But then we'd have to change the name of our place to 'Hobgoblin Creek.'" The thought of this made my stomach hurt.

"Nah. Let's keep it Goblin Creek. It's our place. I don't think they would mind. Plus, I brought them gifts." In Laurel's palm were six or seven coins of various sizes. "Look at these. I'm sure they'll bring us luck."

"Where did you get those?" I asked.

We stood there out of view from the main street inspecting each one of them. I recognized the letters enough to know some were from Mexico, and I believe one said Finland, but the others had characters I had never seen before.

"These are amazing," I said holding each one to inspect their weight, size, and value.

"Thanks," Laurel said, "My dad had some old coins he let me have. I think he got them from the days that he traveled a lot."

"Does he not travel anymore?"

"No. Not anymore," she said. "He got a job here and wants to stay. Mom and I love having him around more often."

Our feet sunk into the earth, damp from the morning dew.

"Come on," I said. "Let's get to the hideout."

From there we traveled further up the creek, behind many unsuspecting backyards, until the path opened up to a field.

The hobgoblins had performed their magic: the willow tree stood a hardy stone's throw from the creek in an opening of wild grass. Its branches touched the ground like my arms did when I laid on my belly on my bed, my fingers gently playing with the carpet fibers at the beginning of the day.

The young leaves of grass tenderly stretched from the earth, unaware of anyone watching yet enjoying their newfound freedom from the dormant ground. The leaves of the willow tree had barely emerged, not quite showing off their true, full-leaf glory, but it was clear—magical creatures had been here.

Laurel and I ran to the tree, inspecting the ground around it before parting the budding curtains to enter. Inside, Laurel placed her mat on a dry patch to sit and pulled out her coins again. After inspecting each once again, I stood up and marched five paces north, then two paces east—making sure to compensate for any length of stride gained from my winter growth spurt. I knelt down, opened my backpack that was half full of snacks and notebooks for the day, and pulled out a small hand shovel. I dug down in that exact spot to reveal a metal box.

"You found it!" Laurel exclaimed.

I walked back over to the trunk where Laurel was already halfway through with her coke. The second I sat down next to her, we had the box open.

"Oh my goodness," she exclaimed, pulling out a *Bop* magazine from two years before, we had wrapped it in plastic to preserve it, yet some of the edge looked damp. "I can't believe I liked Jonathan. He looks so weird in this picture."

"What are you talking about? I remember you wanted to marry him," I said.

"That's not true," she began to defend herself before finding the plastic, machine-bought rings we got on our way home from a movie.

"Remember?" she asked laughing, "remember when we got these and that lady thought they were real?"

"She thought we stole them," I exclaimed. "She couldn't believe we were old enough to own something so nice."

"Little did she know." Laurel smiled.

We laughed at the contents of the box for as long as there was stuff to gawk over before putting our new treasures inside: six various-sized coins from around the world.

"Do you think the goblins will take them?" I asked, forgetting our conversation about hobgoblins.

"Why wouldn't they?" she answered. "But I don't think they will take them soon. Look at the creek." Laurel pointed to the creek, and it was clear the water was too high and the hobgoblins too busy this time of year to collect their gifts.

Through most of the late spring and into summer, the creek had slow moving water. When the water was shallower, it appeared to be green. The two of us loved to imagine a world of enchantment living under the creek, making the waters that color. We could never see what they were doing, but we liked to think they were always watching.

"What do you think the goblins do all winter?" I asked. "Do you think they hibernate, or do they travel somewhere warm to live?"

"I think they are always down there," Laurel said throwing a rock and watching it splash in the fast current. "They like to keep things in order."

As the spring turned into summer, the willow tree's curtains brought us shelter from the sun. I would bring my radio and an extra set of D batteries so we could listen to the latest pop songs. Laurel would bring a new *Tiger Beat* magazine, and we would dream about Freddie Prince Jr., Justin Timberlake, or Christian Bale all the while drinking our soda through Red Vine licorice straws. Mainly, I would imagine my movie star career and my handsome celebrity husband, and Laurel would daydream of making films that would change the world.

This was our favorite way to spend our summer. Who knows where those dreams disappeared to? Perhaps I decided that there was more to life than just the dream of twinkling lights of Hollywood, but I believe Laurel's dream was for real. I knew she would have changed the world if only she could have lived a little while longer.

I didn't realize what that place meant to me until Laurel stopped coming as often. It was the summer before our eighth-grade year. Sometimes I went alone to Goblin Creek, but if she couldn't come, I just preferred to lock myself in the cool basement and watch a rented video. I got really frustrated with her when she would tell me she couldn't come.

"My mom won't let me come today," she told me over the phone.

I wrapped that telephone coil around my finger so many times the tip would turn purple. "What do you mean? You haven't been able to come all week," I said.

It was silent on the other end. Finally, she whispered, "I know."

I couldn't imagine what I was doing so wrong to make her not want to hang out with me. Did her parents think I was a bad influence? Did she have other friends, another life, a boyfriend she wasn't telling me about?

She told me she had to go, and that was it. That was all I heard from her that week.

The following week, we met at my house and walked out of the neighborhood, up Vine Street, cut through the Presbyterian church's parking lot. The awkwardness was thick. Each step was calculated and each word was met with a sideways glance. I didn't want to do or say anything that would take my best friend away. Until we reached the willow.

"I have an extra bag of Cheese Puffs if you want it," I said, trying to be as natural as possible but falling short.

Laurel gazed through the canopy to the creek. She waned a smile and said, "No, thank you."

"I brought water, too," I said in a desperate attempt to give her something that would make things normal again. Perhaps she liked healthier choices now; I didn't know.

She shook her head.

I tried one last time to offer her something before she interrupted.

"I have cancer," she said. "My cancer is out of remission."

I stood there. I had heard grownups talk about cancer before, but Laurel wasn't a grown up. I also knew she was sick before arriving in Utah, but I didn't realize—

"So, it wasn't something I did?" I asked feeling my lungs expand with new air.

"Did? You didn't give me cancer," Laurel shook her head, confused.

"No—" My voice stuck in my throat. "No, I mean—you're not mad at me?"

Laurel displayed a wry smile and then settled in, curling over her legs with a sigh.

"I thought that was why you were avoiding me," I said.

"No. Never. No way." And then she was back. "No, I've had a lot of tests done this week. I couldn't say anything until we were sure."

At the time, I had no way to comprehend all that she had to do. Laurel taught me what leukemia does to the body, and how radiation worked. I had no idea *what* chemo did or what the phrase "out of remission" actually entailed. I didn't know that each time a person's cancer came back, the harder it was to fight.

When school started, Laurel didn't return. Her parents were concerned about her getting sick from the kids there, but they would let her come over still. On the days that we could, we would sneak back to our willowy sanctuary, but many days she just asked to watch a movie at the house, and then my dad would drive her home.

Soon she didn't come to my house at all, and I spent some afternoons during the week with her in her room since she didn't feel like doing much. But we yearned to go back to Goblin Creek—to our willow, feel our feet in the dirt. We wanted to see what our magical friends had done while we had been away. What colors did they put on display?

Laurel became gaunt, her hair thinned until her parents threw a party and shaved it. I considered shaving my head too, but I didn't. I'm not really sure why. It was confusing how happy everyone was when my friend was dying. People brought her gifts, and her house was always decorated like it was her birthday with balloons and banners. Even my parents took me out to dinner more often and let me chose where we ate. It was like everyone was pretending nothing bad was going on—or perhaps overcompensating. I just wanted people to act normal.

Winter came, and I imagined how the tree looked in the snow. Sometimes a winter storm in Utah would give us three feet of snow that would cancel school and allow us a snow day to play outside, but that year, whatever trace of snow that fell didn't last long. Laurel was really sick, so she couldn't go out much anyway. I ventured out to the willow tree every couple of weeks just to check on things. That winter, I found the ground barren and hard. The creek had all but dried up, and the branches of our willow tree had nothing to give; it gave no shelter and its lifeless limbs whipped in the wind instead of gliding with it. What kind of trick were these hobgoblins playing? Why did they take so much away in such a short time? The ground beneath it was too frozen to even draw my name in the dirt. Cold and rejected, I went home.

When I arrived home, my mom sat down on the couch next to me. I had been trying to eat some mini pizzas, but they had already gone cold. I wasn't hungry anyway.

"Hi, Darling, how are you doing?" she asked putting her hand on my knee.

"Fine." I responded, having started my training in the arts of teenage/parent conversations. It didn't divert her, though.

"I heard from Laurel's mom today," she said.

My silence let her know I was listening.

"Her medication isn't working," she said.

I didn't respond. I didn't know to think. In my head I was screaming at her to stop talking—to not finish what she was saying, but I couldn't get any sound.

Mom paused then said, "Laurel's medication isn't working. The doctors don't know why and they don't know what else to do."

All I wanted was to run back to our tree, to go back to how things were, to laugh and dream again with my friend. But I sat there on my couch, with my mother's arms wrapped around me, weeping.

That was it, then. The leukemia was not giving up. Three months later, on April 6, 1994, Laurel passed away in her home.

The day she died I walked to Goblin Creek. I left our neighborhood, crossed the back parking lot of the Presbyterian Church, climbed the levee, and walked to our place. The ground was muddy and hard to walk in. Our weeping willow looked bare and dismal, and there was no sign of the hobgoblins anywhere. That whole year I had held it together, but when I made it to the willow, I fell to my knees in tears of loss, anguish, and loneliness. I was covered in mud and didn't care.

I cried. I knew she was free of the disease that took her. Yet, I was angry at having such little time with her. We were fourth cousins, after all, shouldn't that count for something? Why take her away and not me—I wasn't the one with a plan; I was the one who didn't know what she was doing.

"I'm not even that good in school!" I exclaimed.

To this day I don't know who I was talking to. The willow? Some hidden magical creatures? God? I didn't care.

I reached into my backpack for my little shovel, paced five steps north, two steps east and began to dig. I used the shovel for a short time before I abandoned it for my hands, and I dug until I got the box. The mud made the box slippery and harder to open, but when it did, I grabbed the coins. By the time I was able to look at them, they were unreadable under the muck from my dirty hands. Dark clouds moved in, and the sky turned black as if the day had never come. I stayed there at Goblin Creek for several hours holding those coins in my hand. I was there by myself, but I didn't feel alone. I felt the eyes of our magical friends watching me, and I imagined that Laurel was there, too. When I was ready, I stood up, walked over to the shallow creek and threw every coin in—value be damned!

"Take 'em!" I screamed, "Take every. Last. One of them." When the last one disappeared beneath the green water, I let out a yell that had been building up for months. When I saw a back porchlight turn on from behind one of those suburban fences, I knew it was time to go.

The next few days were dreary. The dark clouds wept down on all of us without letting up much. It wasn't until the day of her funeral that the sky cleared. I have never seen a sky so clear and blue. Just hours before her funeral, I managed to make it back to Goblin Creek—the hobgoblins had been busy. There were flowers, yellow and white, on the ground that I had never seen there before, and the wild grass was alive. I know that the official first day of spring is the third week of March, but after seeing the creek that day, I declared that day its official first day. Piled at the base of our willow tree were six neatly stacked coins.

I wept silently as I watched Laurel's casket be placed into the ground and family shoveled the dark dirt on top. Laurel was buried in Dawn Cemetery directly underneath a budding willow tree. It was the first time in days that the dark blanket of clouds didn't keep close watch over me and our town. It was the first time in days I was able to see the sky clearly.

11

Tableau

Felicia Rose

Often I wish I could hold
the twilight of morning
stop time, or at least
slow it down.

The moment
that faint frieze
of light
illumines
the mountains
enhalos a landscape
of haystacks in snow.

When the room
calm as a cloister
diffuses a balm
of balsam-fir smoke.

And you, my love,
asleep beneath a quire
of quilts
sigh gently and stir
imbuing the moment
with song.

Someone To Follow

Eric Bishop

MY GROUP SPEAKS ENGLISH, BUT "HAYSTACK," "pillow," and "tongue" mean something different to Grand Canyon boatmen than to a guy raised in the dairy country of northern Utah. I'd floated the San Juan River a year earlier, so I could row—sort of. But that lazy stretch of water had no rapids like this, nor can I leave my private trip.

The chatter continues, and I elbow through.

Seventeen miles after launching at Lee's Ferry, we're perched on a cliff, scouting Houserock Rapid. The river rumbles downstream, taking a sharp right turn. At the corner's apex, a boat-swallowing hole churns next to a bus-sized boulder that's covered with cheese-grater sharp ridges.

"A boat ripper," someone says.

Finally, something I understand.

The men and women point to the hole and the rock. Words like "current" and "wave" give me insight. My stomach heaves, as if the river is inside trying to burst free. I'm moments from rowing my raft, complete with eighteen days of gear and food around haystacks, tongues, and eddies without knowing which is which.

"You can do this." My father's hand rests on my shoulder.

I swallow hard, do it again, and refuse to puke the oatmeal and peaches I'd had for breakfast. A man named Roger approaches. Even through his mirrored aviator glasses, the stare makes me more aware of my inexperience. He looks away, shaking his head in disgust. For a second, his back turns, and I think he'll leave. But then he spins then steps forward. Beneath his hat-dana, the mirrored glasses reflect my image: pale, face drawn, mouth partially open. People flinch as a wave crashes below.

"Rapids do that," somebody explains. "They roar along, building to an explosion."

"You gettin' any of this?" Roger asks. I'm glad his eyes are hidden because his posture and elevated voice do plenty to convey displeasure.

"Little bit." My voice cracks. "Kind of."

Roger sticks out among our group. He's floated the Colorado River through Grand Canyon thirteen times. He's been down Cataract Canyon close to fifty. And most important, Roger has never flipped his raft.

He turns to the river, stomps his sandals and scratches at his beard. He's annoyed, probably even pissed, but he brings to mind a character from an old movie. He's Oddball, played by Donald Sutherland in *Kelly's Heroes*, the hippie tank-driver who saves Clint's ass.

"Do this," he says. "Put your boat three boat-lengths behind mine." Roger shakes three skinny fingers in my face then pauses long enough for the rapid's roar to fill my head. "Do everything you see me do—and hope I don't fuck up!"

Middle aged and lean, Roger strides toward the beach.

Other boatmen, oars in hand, are ready to guide rafts through the first serious rapid. Passengers untie ropes from rocks and tamarisk bushes then push into the calm water above the rapid.

"I think the captain has given us our orders." Dad's smile is obviously meant to man me up.

I nod, and we walk toward the river. Gripping the oars, I notice as people in boats up and downstream buckle their life preservers and help one another cinch straps that had previously been loose. I blush, wondering if anyone noticed that I didn't remove my life preserver to scout the rapid. My father coils our bow-line, buckles up, and launches us.

The first raft plunges downstream ahead of Roger. For an instant, the boatman yanks then pushes his oars before his sixteen foot tubes disappears into the spray beyond the edge. Stroking forward, I estimate three boat lengths but oar too hard and come inches from bumping Roger's stern. Then as I back-paddle, the current accelerates Roger well beyond three boat lengths.

"You heard him, Son," Dad yells over his shoulder from the bow, his voice barely discernable over the crashing water. "Do everything you see him do!"

In two oar-strokes, Roger disappears, and then the current takes us. I'm in the middle of an automatic car wash that douches out my ear canals, sweeps over my knees, and covers my face. I work the oars, catching glimpses of Roger as I try to pinpoint where he is in the rapid so I can mimic at the right time. On the downriver side of a hole, a back-curling wave sends a wall of water over the bow and my father's head. It shows me how it looks from behind as water skier yells, "Hit it!"

Near the bottom, I angle backwards, like Roger. to pull away from the cheese-grater rock. Up close, the hole could swallow me and three more. My boat is now a bathtub full to the brim, and I swear I'm rowing a tank instead of an inflatable.

"Rock over here!"

I yank on unresponsive oars that seem stuck in cement.

"An inch is as good as mile," Dad tells me as we slide past.

"Thanks." I rethink trying to match Roger oar-stroke for oar-stroke then jump on the dry-box and pump my fists in the air. But my victory dance dies when I look down at Dad throwing water from the non-self-bailing raft. And see Roger is helping his wife and son do the same.

Bear Bryant's words to his football players come to me.

"And when you get to the end-zone," the coach told them, "Act like you've been there before."

So, I work the hand-held bilge pump to help return the rest of the water to the river.

"You guys okay?" Roger asks.

"Thanks to you— Captain."

"Goddamn ugly, but you made it." Then he gives me a "That'll do pig" nod. "Let's get out of the eddy and run another one."

That evening over steaks and Dutch-oven potatoes, we relive the adventure. Roger emerges my captain.

"Mind if I follow again?" I ask at the next big rapid.

"Catch me if I fall out." His polite response so different from my first impression and Houserock's F-bomb.

Between rapids, Grand Canyon lifts our eyes as the Colorado's current pushes us around each bend. Days roll together with the June sun darkening our tan-lines. During stretches of flat water, I row close and pepper The Captain with questions about rafts, rivers, dry-boxes, and oars; he patiently answers all.

At Tanner Rapid, I go sideways through a hole. The river moves faster than my boat as I surf and nearly flip.

On day eight, we launch into adrenaline alley, a section with rapids like Hance, Grapevine, and Sockdolager. The waves are bigger, the current faster. And I'm exposed for a hacking, clumsy rookie, slapping at surging water, while The Captain finesses through.

Each night we sleep under the stars, the river lulls us to sleep then becomes the soundtrack of our dreams. We then wake and row to side canyons, visit ancient Hopi murals, shower under waterfalls, and watch the moon and sun rise above canyon walls.

By the time I learn The Captain is a child psychotherapist at Primary Children's Hospital in Salt Lake, my first impression of this man is as far away as New York City.

"I bet he's an amazing therapist," my father offers.

I think about how he coaches me through the rapids, how he tolerates my pestering questions, and picture him counseling grief-stricken children. Having two daughters under age five, I note everything he offers about raising kids.

The night before Grand Canyon's ugliest rapid, Lava Falls, I follow him through the chow line, taking identical portion sizes, mirroring on my plate where he placed the pork-chop and rice on his.

The Captain smiles.

The next morning, I know what he'll do after studying his moves for close to two-hundred miles. An unanticipated current spins his boat ninety degrees. I'm ready and have a cleaner run than my mentor.

The second to last day, The Captain's somber mood makes me wonder if he's grown weary of me. He sips beer on his boat after dinner without speaking. I approach, try to make small talk. His response is polite, but he's withdrawn so I take the hint and leave.

Perhaps I'm a barnacle.

The final morning, I talk with others of ice-cream, fountain drinks, and pizza. The chatter continues at the takeout ramp as we pile gear from rafts onto trucks and trailers.

Then I twist the valves and watch the once-tight tubes deflate. A few yards downstream, The Captain, head bowed, stares at his flaccid raft like he's visiting a sick relative.

And I want to trade all civilizations comforts for another day on the river.

Everyone hugs goodbye, except The Captain, who shakes hands. So I'm surprised when he pulls me close.

"You've earned your wings."

"Thanks, Captain."

He moves across the parking lot and opens his SUV's door.

"Next time," he yells to me before climbing in, "I follow you."

Flipper on Crack

Jeff Bateman

Should be jigging off the bottom a little,
just for appearance's sake, but I don't,
broomstick pole sits stiff on the gunwale.

Halibut fishing's like bait fishing trout,
only fun after the strike and you don't look cool doing it.
It's what you do when you limit out on Salmon.

Not that I wasn't in near complete bliss.
Favorite Macanudo cigar in my mouth,
sleepy sunshine after a cold Canadian morning,
Dead calm, flat inland sea. Peace.

And the smell of salt air, savored deliberately,
like little tastes of a childhood on Puget Sound,
Dad's fishing hoody, oysters in the raw, catching Dungeness
with a rake.

Two bumps at the end of the broomstick. Slight. Tap tap.
Could be a snag, just watch, wait. Tap tap.
I clench my cigar in my teeth, I want to keep it,
but setting a hook is a two handed deal. Dilemma.

I've seen guys fish with a cigar or pipe, even tie on flies.
Not me. I either go blind from the smoke, burn myself, or choke
on some gross tobacco backwash.
Still, I clench the cigar, until I know for sure I'm in a fight.

Nothing subtle about hooking a halibut.
Slack in, start at the water, yank it to your head, hope for the
best.
Halibut don't run when hooked, heavy is all you feel.

They call the big ones "Doors," cause they look like one,
little ones "Chickens," for perfect eating size,
something people say when they don't catch a door,
like catching minnows and calling 'em pan sized.

No fight in this fish on the long reel up,
is this a log? A Ling cod?

Dark shape up through the green tinted sea, flash as the fish
sees me,
white as she turns over, her belly exposed, diving.
White runs on, like the end of an old movie reel.

Broomstick smacks the gunwale hard, reel spits line, down she
goes,
taking all I just cranked in.

Buddy Jim on autopilot, tackle in, engine up, deck clear for the
fight to come,
yelling, "big damn fish" over and over.

She stops running, reel like crazy, bring her up again,
we spy her whole length before she runs,
Jim jumping up and down, "Jeezus! Big Fish. Big Fish!"

Third time up. I'm smoked. Left arm so pumped I can't
straighten it.
Jim offers help, but I'd have to hand my man card over with the
broomstick.
I tell him I'm good. Hope she doesn't run again.

The fish slips towards the surface, past where she turned before,
into shallow water.
Alongside now, big as the bottom of the boat.
Jim looks at me. "No harpoon. I'm really sorry."

Look down at the prize we won't get to keep. Can't drag her
without a harpoon,
can't bring her in the boat, even a "chicken" is dangerous in a
boat.
Think about looping a line through her gills maybe,
but she's not tired now, frothing the water, Flipper on Crack.

Cut her loose close to the hook, she slips backwards, gone in a
single kick.
Sitting in stunned silence, spent,
I spot my cigar, floating by like a turd.

Jim's crushed, but not me.

Had the fight of my life, my old man and the sea.
She'll lay millions of eggs, more "butts" to catch.
That's what you say when your "door" gets away.

I breathe deep on the ride to shore,
storing saltwater memories.

At San Clemente's Beach

Marilyn Ball

It is dark over the Pacific.

Circles of mist bath palm tree fronds
nodding in surrender to the boom
of long lipped surf's mysterious,
perpetual rhythm.

The water and I seek shore, waves
rolling, thinning into foam dimple
sand banks, rolling back
with the moon's steady pull.

I know we are bound by our own
deliberations—finding sunlight, shadows,
rolling with our choices, giving our souls their own
     rhythms to catch
waves of life to ride them out and on.

A November Drive

Marilyn Ball

The Kaibab is the near desert's hoard
of ponderosa pine: regal green
splashed with heavy snow.
We know that Grand Canyon's crevice
is deep and quiet, flakes drifting icy white.
I stop to hear wind music tear at pine boughs
leaving them to wave at winter in their world.

Ravens waddle near, share North Rim,
squawking, beg for food, legs atwitter.
We are here to walk the Rim of the Grand,
see deeply this land, its dark ridges and rock,
cold with winter's first snow: see
Angel's Landing in today's first sun,
note God's handiwork, marvel at one more
creation we can hoard by camera and heart.

The Little Bear

Jennifer Sinor

For Michael

WE PUT in at a bend on the Little Bear River. While the boys chased a marmot back into its hole on the steep banks, Michael and I wrestled the canoe from the top of the van. Mid-April in northern Utah, the temperature dropped ten degrees each time the sun slipped behind a cloud. Daffodils and crocus dotted the sides of the busy road, bobbing in the breeze. When I looked toward the Wellsville Mountains, I could see a raft of cloud heading our way and wished I had packed our fleece jackets.

The green canoe was awkward and heavy, and I tried to balance it on my head as we moved away from the van.

"You got it?" Michael asked when the canoe wobbled like a drunk.

I didn't answer, just swung it from my head to the ground, one swift motion that took all my strength. Once it was down, we began to drag it to the river.

"Put your life jackets on," I called to the boys as I loaded the canoe with the cooler, blankets, and paddles. Aidan and Kellen ignored me, poked sticks into the marmot's hole instead. "Life jackets," I said again, a spring gust taking my words.

Michael and I slid the canoe down the steep bank, rocks and gravel rolling under our feet. We were putting in just south of the bridge where the road crossed the river, and I could see abandoned swallow's nests fastened to the concrete. The swallows had yet to return for the season, but the red-winged blackbirds called from the brush, high-pitched shrieks and trilling whistles, a welcome and familiar chatter, one of the first signs of spring.

"You know," I said to Michael, "you should wear the other life jacket, not me. If anything were to happen, you would need to help us."

Michael guided the canoe into the water like he might return a trout to the river, channeling the body through his long fingers, slowing the slide.

"You wear it," he said, as he steadied the canoe against the shore. Then he turned to call the boys. "Aidan and Kellen, hop in. It's time to go."

And because it was cold and the life jacket would be one more layer, and because the canoe was already pulling to be off, and because the boys needed help boarding the boat, and because I knew that we were only wearing the life jacket to set an example, I zipped it on, the vest a welcome embrace.

Once aboard, we floated quickly under the bridge, the river wide and muddy. On the shore, trees in early leaf stretched over the water, forming a tunnel through which we passed. I sat in front, a paddle resting at my feet, while the boys, seven and five, sat on the bottom of the boat. The two-person canoe meant they didn't have seats but rather camped on a wool blanket that must have felt both warm and scratchy against their bare legs.

Michael paddled from his seat in the back, gentle J-strokes that kept us in the middle of the current. When I turned to look at him, he smiled, the easy smile he always had for the natural world, as if by leaving behind the van he had come home.

Fifteen years earlier, before we had boys, or a van, or any of those tethers that cause you to go to bed early so you can face carpools, sack lunches, and endless whining, Michael and I canoed our *Green Heron* down the gentle waters of the Huron River. We would put in at sunset, when the Michigan sun punctured thick stands of maple and picnicking families packed up to go home. A bottle of wine, sometimes two, a paper bag stuffed with bread and cheese from the local deli, and two wooden paddles were our only gear. Michael would recite poetry from memory, Pattiann Rogers or Mary Oliver, as he navigated the wide channel. His choices grew more boisterous as we drank, so that an hour and a half into the trip he would be flinging Pound's "Winter Is Icumen In" or Larkin's "This Be the Verse" toward the stars. I loved that he knew poems by heart, that he carried Blake and Shakespeare and Dickinson with him, fleets of words he set to sail on the river, our canoe buoyed by metaphor and image and voice. I, on the other hand, had memorized my day planner, could name the aisle in the local grocery where you would find Cheerios, knew to the penny the amount in my bank account, as well as the seven ingredients found in the Seafood Pita Pocket I sold as a teenager when I worked fast food. Because Michael brought art into the natural world, it meant every hike, every canoe trip, every backpack became laced with lines in pursuit of the transcendent. Our canoe, both boat and metaphor.

Usually at least once on our night floats down the Huron, often when the last shreds of light appeared like window panes between tree trunks, we would round a bend in the river and surprise a great blue heron. Prehistoric and heavyset, the giant bird would take off from its perch, tucking its claw-like feet against its body, and move slowly into the air, annoyance in every beat of its wings. Seemingly to make a point, it would often oar toward us, low over our heads, and then turn downstream to roost once more. A moment later, another bend, and the same heron would take flight again. We repeated the pattern several times, could anticipate the feathered whoosh of air above our heads, until, at last, the dinosaur of a bird flew upstream rather than down, leaving us in the Michigan night.

We would remain silent in the canoe for a long time; not even poetry could capture such encounters.

As we floated down the Little Bear, April sun lost behind clouds and the yellow-headed blackbirds sounding their alarm, I thought of those many canoe trips. How Michael courted me with poetry and rivers, so that his veined heart became the channel I followed, how we heaved the canoe and our drunken bodies up the shore and lay in the heron-plumbed blackness looking for the moon, how we never imagined we might, fifteen years later, paddle the same canoe down a western river with our boys (hearts now outside our bodies), sitting between us. In Michael's smile, his easy strokes, those rivers all ran together, so that this moment in the spring sunshine, quiet babble of boys, drill of bird, bob of tree branch, unfolded under the same "bones of the sky," "the meticulous layering" not of down but of memory, Rogers's redbird right there with us.

"Who's ready for lunch?" I called and reached for the cooler, unzipping the top.

"Me! Me!" Kellen shouted. He rose on his knees and the canoe wobbled, his forty pounds enough to shift the boat.

"Whoa," said Michael, "Careful." I watched him switch the

paddle to the other side of the boat to stabilize the rock. "No sudden movements."

Aidan reached to pull Kellen back to the floor of the boat. "You're gonna tip us."

As usual, Kellen ignored his older brother and held out his hand for a slice of cheese, though I noticed he stayed more still this time. I passed Aidan a wedge of cheddar as well as some crackers and a small bunch of purple grapes. "Share."

Michael and I only tipped our canoe once, during our trip to Algonquin Provincial Park in Canada. We had headed to the waters to celebrate the completion of Michael's PhD, the *Green Heron* strapped to the top of his Honda Accord, our clothes and food stuffed into rented dry bags.

The McKaskill Lake Ranger Cabin sits in a stand of red pine on a peninsula deep inside the park boundaries. To make our way there, we would have to put in at the Shall Lake Access Point and then paddle across several large bodies of water, as well as portage the canoe for miles between lakes. Because Michael had been busy defending his dissertation, we had not done the research necessary for such a long trip. Had we, we would have realized that such a journey calls for a light, kevlar canoe, something one person could carry easily on his shoulders. We arrived at the park entrance at dusk, our heavy fiberglass canoe atop the car.

Because we had already driven two days, and because we had no money to rent a kevlar canoe, we camped by the trail-head and set out early the next morning. At first, the two of us carried the canoe by the handles at either end, our dry bags the cargo. But my arms quickly grew tired and the progress was slow because we had to keep stopping in order for me to switch hands. As the sun vaulted the noon hour, we grew worried that we wouldn't make the cabin by nightfall. For the rest of the day,

Michael carried the *Green Heron*, all seventeen feet of it, on his shoulders, plus a dry bag on his back. Mosquitoes swarmed his face and neck, their black bodies dark against his skin. He didn't have a hand to swat them away, so they feasted on his arms, his neck, the soft skin below his ears. Scrambling behind with the other dry bag, trying not to trip on root and rock, I could hear Michael pant from the exertion. He didn't talk, didn't make a sound. August heat pressed like wet washcloths to our faces. One foot in front of the other, five hundred yards, a mile, then canoe across open water, then shoulder the burden again.

I didn't think we would make it, couldn't see how Michael could keep going, but eventually we arrived at McKaskill Lake and canoed across the water to our cabin. I knew it was bad when Michael suggested feigning a broken leg so that a helicopter could take us back out.

Those days at the isolated cabin were amazing, though, a refuge amid miles of old-growth forest, trees that took root when Shakespeare was alive. Every night we fell asleep to the ghostly call of loons and listened to the moose forage outside our windows. During the day, we hiked or paddled around the remote lakes, drinking unfiltered water through cupped hands. The day before we left, we tipped the canoe, right at the shore when we were climbing out for a picnic lunch.

"We should never have tried to board when it was crosswise to the shore," Michael said, as we stood, completely shocked and soaked in knee-deep water. "That was dumb." But we laughed because it was only water and the cabin was close and soon we would be dry in front of the roaring fire.

I didn't think about Algonquin as we headed down the Little Bear, though we sat in the same canoe that Michael had carried. Instead, I studied the light, how, when the sun did appear, the water, the leaves, the birdwing seemed illumined from within. I didn't worry about tipping or trekking or becoming soaked. On the drive to the Little Bear from our house, earlier that morning, I had realized that such freedom from danger and worry was a gift Michael had given me for years. He mentioned, as we drove to the Little Bear, that he wanted to check the conditions at both the put-in and take-out sites. In my head, I thought about how much Michael worried, too much, and how everything was always just fine. A moment later, though, I realized that I didn't have to worry because he always did. My peace of mind was a privilege. That I could float down the Little Bear handing out a picnic was possible only because Michael took responsibility for everything else.

Up ahead, the river bent. From where I sat the river appeared to end altogether, the turn was so sharp. I knew at some point we would float under a great blue heron rookery, and I imagined for a moment seeing one of the giant birds rise from the shore as we made the turn. The bird would be larger than either Aidan or Kellen, with a wingspan as long as five feet. Perhaps it would be holding a fish in its beak, waiting to gulp the silvery body in one piece down its elegant S-shaped neck. It would sweep across our heads, belly just feet above us, bearing both its lunch and our past.

As we approached the bend, though, I forgot about herons. The river grew shallow on the inside of the turn. I could see the round rocks on the bottom, green and coppery in the sun.

"Michael," I called. "It's too shallow. We need to move to the right."

I didn't like shallow water. Just the week before we had run aground in the Cutler Marsh and had to extricate ourselves from the muddy bottom. I was worried we would ground ourselves here in six inches of water, jam the rocker into the sludgy bottom. But I hardly had time to articulate that thought to myself let alone name the fear aloud when the current picked up and we swung around the bend, the calm river replaced with white water.

It was as if there were two different rivers. The one before the turn and the one after. What had been wide, shallow, and slow moving funneled into a narrow chute. What had been straight and easily navigable became a lightning-shaped series of turns. To our right, at the first tight bend, a giant poplar had toppled into the river, its crown and trunk blocking the river. Branches and limbs reached across our path and formed a cage. We were headed straight for it.

Michael didn't ask me to paddle. He was too busy thrusting his own paddle into the water. I threw down the knife and chunk of cheese, grabbed the paddle. Within two strokes, though, I knew we were going to crash.

The morning we left our cabin in Algonquin, I recalled the temperature of the water when we had fallen in. Shelter and a fire had been close by, so our shivering matched our laughing as we ran for warmth. A storm threatened our departure, and I could feel the chill in the air. We could see the dark clouds gathering to the north of us, throbbing masses of gray, but we set out anyway, knowing we had to be back in Ann Arbor the following day. It wasn't until the final crossing, the largest stretch of water, that the storm really hit. As we had navigated the trails, Michael once again bearing the canoe on his back, and then oared the crossings, the hemlock and yellow birch around us swayed in the gusts, some rain making it through the thick canopy to land on our heads and shoulders. Now, though, the trees blurred together in the wind, sugar maple becoming hemlock, the forest thrashing like a many-headed monster. Rain and wind swept against us, somehow rising from our feet, air and ground no longer meaningful, the world turned into storm. Even if the other shore had been close enough to see, we would have been unable to trace its outline through the mess. Waves crested on the lake, white caps crashing into one another, a turning brew of water that merged with the wind and rain. No one else was around, the middle of the day as dark as night, hardwood trees thin lines of black around us.

"We'll go at an angle," Michael said.

My teeth chattered even though it was August, my shirt and shorts soaked as thoroughly as they had been the morning before when we tipped.

"We can't go straight across," he continued. "The waves will tip us. So we'll have to cut through them at an angle. We'll head north of our landing place and then cut back south with the wind and waves behind us."

Michael stood, the canoe on the ground near his feet, and motioned our path with his hand. Our dry bags sat between the yokes where he had strapped them down with bungees. Water ran down his face, rain most likely but also sweat from having carried the canoe so far already that day. He didn't even try to wipe it away. Instead he gazed out at the lake, calculating, I knew, how to navigate.

"Once we commit," he said, "you need to keep your head down and paddle as hard as you can. Don't look up. Don't stop. Just paddle with everything you've got."

I didn't need to ask him about the dangers. I knew from his tone that they were many and varied and most of them ended up with us going into the lake with our gear.

Head down and paddle, I thought, as I helped Michael push the canoe into the raging water.

Every stroke resulted in little forward movement. The winds thrashed against us, our canoe a prop on the stage of storm. I couldn't see the shore, only saw dark water capped with frenzied white, but I trusted Michael to carry us there. I kept my head down and paddled, short hard strokes, quick and powerful. The canoe pitched and tossed, pulled or guided I couldn't tell, but I just counted my stokes. Ten on this side. Ten on the other. Again and again. Short, deep, fast.

"Hit the deck," I yelled, dropping the paddle, and I threw myself to the bottom of the boat, taking the boys to the floor with me.

The front of the canoe plunged into the cage of limbs, where we stuck.

"I'm scared. I'm scared," Aidan started crying. And then Kellen, "I want to go home."

Chaos in the *Green Heron* as I looked up to see that Michael was bracing his arms against the limbs to keep the rest of the boat from being pushed further into the tangle of the downed tree. Water rushed past us, almost brimming the gunwales: birdsong replaced by the thunder of spring runoff.

"Michael, pull us out of here. Pull us out of here," I yelled. From my position on the bottom of the boat, underneath the yoke so I could hold the boys, I could only see a roof of limbs above us. The water churned beneath the boat. I could feel the madness through the fiberglass hull. The river wanted the boat; all pressure bent in that direction, into the tree, into the river, down.

"Break some branches," Michael yelled above the fray. "Someone is going to be impaled."

I tried. I used my foot, my hands, all I had, but I couldn't break even the smallest of the limbs. It was a big tree; the river had already taken anything dainty or thin.

"Michael, get us out!" I cried.

He continued to brace his arms against the limbs, trying to

back the canoe against the pull of water edging us forward, but we didn't move at all. There was no way back.

The boys were panicked now, crying and begging to leave the boat. I couldn't see their faces to reassure them, couldn't turn my body around.

"Michael, you have to stop and think. You have to be the one to free us." I could see his face, the strain of his arms against the thick branch. I looked at his eyes, which weren't panicked but purposeful.

"The only way out is through," he yelled. "We have to go through."

Which is what the river wanted, to carry everything with it on its journey north. I looked at the thicket before us and could not see a path.

Undaunted, Michael began to weave the canoe through the cage of bare limbs, using his arms to push against the tree limbs and moderate our exit. But nothing was gentle in the river, nothing slow, nothing quiet. We surged against the crown of the tree, ducking branches and limbs, Michael guiding us as best he could from behind. Never once had he left his place on his seat. The three of us cowered at the bottom of the boat, but he stayed where he was, worked the limbs like a puzzle.

We popped free on the other side of the poplar, the canoe bursting into the rapids. I scrambled to my seat, grabbed the paddle once again. Our speed increased with our freedom. We didn't even cheer our escape. Now back on the main part of the river, still in the narrow, twisted chute, the current took us up again, a dropped stitch, a forgotten plaything, the third strand of a braid. Within seconds, the river swept the canoe into the second turn where the limbs of a bushy willow reached into the river.

"Short strokes," Michael yelled. "Short strokes."

It was the last thing I heard before the canoe tipped over.

The fall before we went to Algonquin, Michael and I took the *Green Heron* up north to the Au Sable Forest to canoe Rifle River, a sixty-mile stretch of water in northern Michigan that is popular for canoes because there are no dams or portages. We camped along the banks under an October sky compressed to the brilliance of a gemstone. Days before the trip, I had told Michael that I loved him for the first time. I could not help but read the carnival of color that surrounded us—maples in every shade of orange and red, birch like flames, honeyed cotton-woods, yellow ash, all backed by the cloudless blue sky—as a celebration of my happiness. On our third afternoon, we put in a few miles up from our tent site. Even though it was the second weekend in October, we wore short sleeves and hats. The sun warmed my skin. Michael sat in the back and paddled while we made our way down the lazy river. Curled leaves in yellows and red, tiny boats, floated alongside us, spinning in the current.

"Let's do that too," Michael said, when I pointed out the leaf armada.

I looked at him, confused.

But then he took his paddle and placed it on the bottom of the boat. Carefully he stood up and stepped over the yoke closest to him.

"Come on," he said.

Realizing what he meant, I waited for him to lay his long body on the bottom of the canoe. Even though the length from bow to stern was seventeen feet, the inside dimensions were much smaller, so Michael's body stretched almost from the back seat to the front. But the *Green Heron* was wide, a stable canoe meant for easy travel, and there was plenty of room beside him. I got up carefully and made my way to his side.

Then the two of us lay in the bottom of the *Green Heron*,

blue sky above, the occasional burst of color as we passed maples and gums, curled fists of leaf falling through the sky, the canoe, bearing the two of us, bobbing down the river, bumping a bush, a limb, the shore, spinning in the water, just like the fleet of leaves surrounding us, the whole world adrift under an October sun.

When I came up, I saw Michael first. He held onto the overturned canoe with one hand and Kellen with the other. Aidan was closest to me, and I reached for him. We were soaked and already panting from fear. The shore rushed past us as we headed down the river, the four of us moving as one.

"You're okay. You're okay," Michael reassured. I didn't look at his eyes to know whether he thought this was true. Instead, I counted our four bodies again and watched the shore fly past.

"You're okay. You're okay," he repeated like a mantra.

Aidan and Kellen's eyes were wide with fear. They gulped both air and water but said nothing. Whereas before, in the cage of limbs, they had cried out in panic, now, faced not with the possibility of danger but danger itself, they conserved their strength and kept their heads above the water.

After a microsecond, I felt the cold pour into my body. The river stole into my jeans and long-sleeved shirt, soaked into my socks and shoes, weighted me down. It felt like the river was inside me, that my very center had gone watery and cold.

Our breaths came faster now. Short, gasping puffs. Our bodies swung around the bend, the shore maybe ten feet away.

"Swim to the shore," I yelled. And I tried to make my voice confident and strong as the rush of water pounded in our ears, blocking every sensation except for cold. I wanted Aidan and Kellen to think we knew what to do, wanted them to trust that we would fix this. But even as I yelled for them to swim, I saw the shore streaming past and wondered how we would make it.

I took Aidan and pushed him in front of me, knowing Michael would take Kellen. Together, we began swimming for land. The rocks and branches were going by so quickly, I worried we wouldn't be able to grab anything. Even if we made it to the shore, I thought the current would slam us against the rocks or that a branch might take out an eye.

We got closer, the force of the current lessening as we grew closer to land. I could taste the mossy water as it splashed my face and mouth, felt the freezing drops on my lips and cheeks.

"Grab on," I cried, hoping that Aidan wouldn't hit serrated metal or sharp rocks, but willing to take blood for land.

"Pull yourself up."

Aidan reached for a rock and then another. I saw him set his feet against the bank. With slow movements, he slowly climbed from the river, and I followed, struggling against the pull of the freezing water. Every time I tried to place my feet down, the current would steal my footing. The rocks on the shore, chunks of concrete really, were hard and jagged, but I welcomed the solidity. I crawled from the water and then looked back for Kellen. Michael was pushing him up the bank only feet from me. With each shove, Michael's head dipped down into the water. It was then that I remembered Michael didn't have a life jacket. While the rest of us bobbed on the river's surface, Michael had held onto the canoe for support. I watched as he struggled to boost Kellen up, the other hand still holding the *Green Heron.*

Michael looked up at me as Kellen made his way to my side. Holding the canoe, he was in the water, five feet below me, his face white with cold.

"Let the canoe go, Michael," I called.

Aidan and Kellen shivered at my sides, my clothes sucked

into my body, the sky now full of cloud. Michael looked up at me.

Then again, louder, "You have to let it go."

I watched him hesitate, watched him look once more at the *Green Heron* overturned in the water, half sunk. Then he let it go. It hurried away, the cooler, his wallet, our water bottles, and our paddles chasing quickly behind.

Maybe the reason Michael recites poetry whenever we are in the natural world, rather than, say, when doing the dishes or taking out the trash, is to attempt to narrate, to hold within the bounds of language, a kind of beauty, joy, fear that we will never completely understand. Much like love itself. Lines of poetry, image and metaphor, frame the encounter, just for a moment, pin down what shifts and changes before our eyes. The mountains, the woods, the rivers, never fully known, yet familiar in the ways they call to us, are caught in image. Suppose your father was a redbird, Pattiann Rogers proposes. Suppose that before you knew how to speak you knew the "slow spread of his wing." "Then," the poet continues,

> you would be obligated to try to understand
> What it is you recognize in the sun
> As you study it again this evening
> Pulling itself and the sky in dark red
> Over the edge of the earth.

Language fails us in both love and beauty; yet it's all we have.

I don't think it is happenstance that Michael and I fell in love under the flap of a heron's wings. Every river runs with certainty toward an ocean that will always accept it, and a canoe follows every turn. All you need to know about love, the fierce ties that bind us as well as the branches that will take you down, can be found between those shores.

The four of us stood on the banks of the Little Bear under a sunless sky. Wind whipped against our wet bodies. Michael had lost his glasses and couldn't see. The canoe and everything with it was gone.

"It doesn't matter what we lost," Kellen said, the first words any of us spoke, uttered as he watched his favorite hat and green water bottle sail down the river. "The important thing is that we all survived."

And that was, of course, true. It's indeed what I felt standing on the bank, the four of us holding onto one another, the boys without shoes, Michael unable to see, water streaming from our clothes. We had made it.

Later I would realize we had only been on the water for fifteen minutes before the canoe turned over; it felt like I had been paddling much longer, that we had lived our lives within the hull of the *Green Heron*. Shock set in and I would only vaguely remember walking for thirty minutes through a cow pasture full of mud and manure, each of us with one boy in our arms, falling repeatedly into pools of filth. We eventually made it back to the van and then home for hot showers and food. The following day Michael would return to the Little Bear to look for the canoe. After two solid days of searching, through bracken and thicket, bruises and abrasions up and down his arms, he would find it, wedged underneath a willow, still upside down.

He would enter the freezing water once again, this time held fast by a rope, and with the help of two friends, pull the *Green Heron* to shore. Aidan will stand on the banks and watch the resurrection because we will want him to know that what is lost can be found. Kellen, though, will refuse to go, will have nightmares every night for weeks, will whimper in his sleep. And that will seem about right to me as well. I too will relive the moment when the world became water and the river ran through me, will spin alternative endings with boys trapped by the yoke, separated from us, Michael unable to keep afloat in the brew. Through my sons, I will hold terror and joy in my hands, left and right, one and the other.

When Michael returns home with the *Green Heron* atop the car, spring rains coming down hard so that both he and Aidan are drenched to the skin, I will run from the house to meet him. His smile will say everything, joy pulsing with rain down his face. And I will hug him to me, feel the rain and the river soak into my sweatshirt as well as the deeper warmth and solidity.

Excerpted from *Sky Songs: Meditations on Loving a Broken World* by Jennifer Sinor by permission of the University of Nebraska Press.

17

Under Water
Brock Dethier

Skiskate the length of Hyrum Lake,
a frosted cucumber from the air,
Little Bear River its stem.
Avoid augured holes,
head for far shore,
swing wide around the inlet
if the ice is dicey.
Magpies will console
if the eagles are away.

The surface is always familiar, always different,
from glide to glide, shore to shore,
year to year. Snow on ice
sometimes milky, sometimes clear,
scoured, packed, patterned by wind,
sun melting crystal for rework,
morning's hoar growing on ice breath.
Skis scrape hard pack

or swish through ice ferns,
pulverizing delicate beauty.

Skate the river stem if there's enough snow.
Watch for mush along the edges--
step big into the middle from the bank.
Follow the bends south, toward the mountains.
Watch for barn owl and beaver,
listen for ducks, whistlers,
below the rapids.
Find a dip in the bank,
sidestep, muscle up
to stand and stare
at the white legs of swamp willows,
calcium ring at eye level,
and realize where you are.

18

Eastward in Eden

Matthew Funk

EASTWARD IN EDEN, on a green hill overlooking a valley in the Bear River range of the Rocky Mountains, there flows a small waterfall.

Not far from the waterfall, my ancestral home presides over our family farm, sheltered beneath hundred-year old elm and catalpa trees. My great-grandfather settled the land the year before Utah was granted statehood in 1896. Victoria was queen of England and Empress of India and that year a twenty-one year old Winston Churchill was a war correspondent filing dispatches for the *Morning Post* from Havana about the Cuban insurrection.

In spring, the newly melted snow cascades over the rocks and, in the cool serenity of the evening, crickets chirp and the smell of my grandma's lilacs floats on the soft breeze.

But in Eden, slithering silently among the rocks and boughs was darkness and sorrow, and as in Eden, so also on the farm. There is a serpent.

It lives in my dresser drawer.

Be it summer or winter, standing in the farmyard as twilight falls is a sublime experience. In June, carried on soft breezes among the trees is the essence of summer—the smell of freshly cut hay and sometimes of sweet rain. The sun's golden light falls like a benediction on the farmstead. In December, as temperatures hover near zero, the cold wind crosses the gloaming and steals my breath as the Rockies turn purple in the waning light. Christmas lights on distant homesteads twinkle in the new-born darkness.

In my dresser, beneath the white athletic socks that haven't been worn in years, below the colorful soft Merino socks I wear to the office, and under the stout gray wool of my winter socks lies a sheaf of papers, evidence of life's struggles and sorrows, testimony of siblings who can no longer stand the sight of one another and generations who died angry at their family.

The oldest of them is a deed executed in 1931; the farm was collateral on a loan to the California Land Bank. Hoover was president and the Great Depression held America in its clenched fist. That spring my great-grandfather Clarence spent virtually all of his capital on a cow he saw at a livestock auction. The cow had excellent conformity and famous bloodlines. It had been brought to Utah all the way from Wisconsin, the beating heart of the American dairy industry.

It was a fraught time. A year earlier the Great Plains were struck by a drought that would bring a new name to Oklahoma: the Dust Bowl. But, combined with great-grandpa Clarence's already excellent herd of Holsteins, this cow's daughters and granddaughters would bring prosperity to our family when other farmers were going hungry. This cow was the future of our dairy and my great-grandfather willingly paid the steep price to buy the animal, sure of success. The future was rich and high in butterfat.

As a boy, I was responsible for feeding and tending to the calves. I was often distracted, usually thinking of the cute cheerleaders in my school when a calf's cough or sniffle would catch my attention. I'd walk through the barn to find the sick animal, and then I'd go find Dad and tell him. Alerting him early to a sick animal was always a sure way to win his approval and affection. If a farmer catches sickness fast, he can usually stop an illness before it spreads through the herd. A sick animal has all kinds of tells, and I became very good at detecting a calf with drooping eyes or uneven breathing or even a tail that wasn't swishing as energetically as expected.

That is why I can imagine with great clarity the chill that struck my Great Grandpa Clarence's heart one morning when his prized cow couldn't stand up. A glance was all it took, and he knew he was in real trouble. The vet was called and the diagnosis couldn't have been worse. Great-grandpa Clarence's newly acquired and very expensive cow had carried brucellosis into the heart of our dairy herd.

Fatal to cattle, brucellosis can also be deadly to humans. When a cow gets brucellosis, there is no cure, no treatment. The animal must be destroyed, immediately. Clarence's cows, his entire herd, had to be put down—at once.

The farm loan came due and great-grandpa Clarence didn't have the five thousand, four hundred and sixty-five dollars to pay it.

It was in this moment, the bank days away from foreclosing on the farm, that great-grandpa Clarence's eldest son—my grandfather, LeRoy—came back to the farm where he'd been raised with six thousand dollars he had scrimped together.

And so the oldest deed in my dresser, dated June 5th, 1931, records the sale of the farm from Clarence to LeRoy. Great-grandpa Clarence moved into a small home in town. His plan was to start again, and he bought a hundred acres of land at a foreclosure sale on the courthouse steps, but that land was bankrupt in more ways than one—it was rocky and hard and perched on a steep hillside; success was elusive. Fifteen years later, he was carried from his small home to the town cemetery.

I've always felt terrible for great-grandpa Clarence. Or maybe what I felt was fear that what happened to him might somehow happen to me. It is only now in mid-life that I can look back and see how that fear of loss controlled my life.

Making a living in the diary business is a lot like walking along the edge of high cliff: on one side lies rocky solidity and on the other a deadly fall to the rocks a thousand feet below. On the one hand is survival, on the other is bankruptcy, shame, and hardship, as my great-grandpa Clarence found out.

My great-grandpa's perils, both economic and physical, must have been evident to him from his earliest memories. For his whole life he knew no other truth. When great-grandpa Clarence was a young boy he suffered the loss of his father, who was killed defending the town against an Indian attack. Great-grandpa Clarence's mother remarried. With two young sons to feed, she had little choice. But the new husband was prone to violent anger, and he beat Clarence often.

One summer night—probably around 1878—when he was about eight-years-old, Clarence's mother woke her two young sons, dressed the boys and quietly led them out of the house while her new husband slept. She hugged her sons goodbye, and then told them to walk the ten miles to a relative's home, where they would be safe.

In my mind I see her, my great-great-grandmother, standing in the night, her arms gripped tightly around herself, watching her two little boys walk into the darkness. It is silent. Not even the crickets chirp.

That was in the late 1870s. By the late 1970s, a farmer's existential threats didn't include Indians, though hail, rain, drought, and disease still threatened.

The image of balancing on the edge of a cliff is very real to me; as a child it was a recurring nightmare. In repeated dreams it is twilight, the sun's golden rays kiss a rocky cliff as I dangle inches away from an endless fall.

One summer evening in the seventies—I was about ten years old—a stranger drove up the lane and parked in the middle of the farmyard. The stranger was a tall man with an easy smile and he spoke with my father as twilight fell. They stood near the iron basketball post Dad had welded for my brothers. Near the basketball standard, my own tiny footprints were captured in the concrete along with the scrawled inscription: *Matt, May 1970.* I was five months old when my feet were pressed into the gray liquid concrete on the morning the basketball post was sunk into the ground.

After speaking with my father for a while, the man left, and I asked my dad what the stranger wanted. Dad said the man wanted to buy our farm. I will never forget the chill that shot straight into my ten-year-old heart upon hearing those words. My world shook a little. I tried to imagine this unthinkable concept: our family without our farm. What would we do, where would we go, what would we even be without our farm? Nothing. We would be nothing. I still remember the sick fear that crashed over me at this horrible thought.

My voice trembled a bit as I casually asked my father if he was going to sell the farm to the stranger. Looking back on that moment, I realize that he could no more sell our farm then he could sell his own heart. Years after, my father had forgotten the man and his presumptuous offer. I remember it. It was the first time I realized that nothing is forever. In looking back on that moment, I think of Ecclesiastes, "To everything there is a season, and a time to every purpose under the heaven."

My footprints are still there in the stone, but decades of wind and rain have made them faint. No one left in my life remembers that May morning.

The next deed in my dresser is dated May 19, 1964. In the thirty-three years since the Great Depression, my grandparents raised three daughters and a son. My grandmother was an exceptional homemaker, known throughout the valley for her sewing and cooking, and there by the waterfall she nurtured the gardens and planted lilacs and elms, maples and pines, catalpas and even a horse chestnut tree that stand tall even now, nearly a hundred years later. My older brother remembers the farm in those days; twenty years ago—when he and I were still speaking —he told me that Grandma's yard was like the jungles of Vietnam, green and lush.

Grandma planted hollyhocks and wild roses that ran along the banks of the creek. I have vivid memories from my childhood of tasting the sweet nectar from the honeysuckle that grew in the shade of the trees. In some of my earliest memories, my father lay on the grass in the cool evenings while I played nearby. Great-grandpa Clarence started the farm, my grandfather LeRoy saved it, and my father, Calvin, more than doubled its size. But of those who came before me, it was perhaps my grandmother who left the most conspicuous mark; she made the farmyard a place of green and peace, of grace and beauty, which is fitting because her name was Grace. My daughters have her eyes and chin.

In 1964, my grandfather gave their home to their son and his wife. My mother avowed that she had warned her husband and his father that they needed to consult Grace before dispossessing her of her home, but they didn't. It must have come as a shock when LeRoy told Grandma that he'd decided it was time to bestow the farm on their son and move into town. Grandma protested—she didn't want to leave her beautiful home and the farmstead—but to no avail; Grandpa's mind was set and in 1964, the farm passed to their son, my father.

But Grandma's plight roused indignation among her daughters. Angry on their mother's behalf and upset that a share of the farm would not pass to them, they stopped talking to their father and brother. I've only met my aunts a handful of times—I'm not even certain I'd recognize them if I passed them in the street. I might have actually done that—as a boy I walked past a woman on the sidewalk that looked like my Aunt Kaye, but her gimlet eye discouraged approach.

Though family histories often say otherwise, rarely do family farms pass from generation to generation without lasting damage to family bonds. As an accountant, I've prepared complicated estate plans dozens of pages long that involve multiple revocable trusts carefully handing a family farm from father to son, only to see the entire plan ripped up barely two weeks later when father and son have their first serious disagreement. I've seen fathers disinherit sons and I've seen fathers ignore wise counsel and rashly transfer their farms to sons, only to be thrown off their land by sons newly freed of their filial obligations.

I did see one farm pass quietly to the next generation; just one. The inheriting son was an only child.

Since Jacob and Esau—well, Cain and Abel, really—human history has been riven with conflict between parents and children and between siblings, not just over inheritance of land, but over what might be the deeper question: who do mom and dad love the most?

To children raised in town, it's perhaps not such an existential question. They're all going to grow up and move out. But for a farmer's children, much hinges on the answer of who is most loved, who is most capable. That child gets to stay in Eden; the other children may come back for holidays if they like.

Of our parents' children, my brother Mike was the one who most needed the farm. This is not to say he loved it the most—we were all pretty equal on that score. But Mom and Dad always urged us to make a living as something other than farmers. They were both college graduates, believed fervently in higher education, and few knew better than my father, third generation farmer that he was, that farm life is a very hard and dangerous life.

Our town's cemetery bears witness to this truth. Scattered among the graves of the very old and very young are granite headstones that hint of tragedy. Several of the headstones mark the graves of boys my age. One marks the resting place of a boy I knew, Kirt Nelson. We played together as children. One summer evening thirty years ago, Kirt fell into a harvester; he was seventeen. Those present still remember the sound of his screams. Not far from Kirt's grave is Kevin Webb's. I didn't know Kevin well; he was six years younger than me. His body was found one June morning pinned under a tractor; Kevin was fourteen.

Kirt and Kevin's deaths were preceded in the decades that came before by other boys and men. In 1969 a tractor rolled over Ron Christensen; he left a bride of four months. Then, in May 1971—my footprints in the cement were barely a year old —Quentin Peart and his son-in-law Dean Smith were killed in a silo accident. Howard Anderson found their bodies. Then in 1972 Howard's boy Troy fell off a truck. Troy was in a coma for six months; eventually he got to where he could feed himself and walk to the bathroom, but he can never be left unattended.

A year later, in 1973, Howard's son Judd fell into a grain auger and lost a leg.

In Ecclesiastes 3:2 the prophet continued enumerating the seasons of life, "A time to be born, and a time to die; a time to plant, and a time to pluck up that which is planted."

My parents' educational admonishments bore fruit, and all six of their children graduated from college. Mike's degree was in agriculture; he wanted to stay on the farm. I wish I could say that there was a happy ending for Mike and his dream of being a farmer, but the next paper in my dresser tells a different tale. It's a notice that the farm mortgage had been paid in full. It's dated February 1997.

In the summer of 1996 Mike was in a motorcycle accident. An hour later he was airlifted to a trauma center in Salt Lake City. Most of us raced to Mike's side prepared to say our good-byes. My father couldn't come—someone had to milk the cows. With the exception of the few weeks in 1931 when Clarence's herd had to be destroyed, the cows on our farm had been milked twice a day without fail for 102 years.

In 1914, the guns of August bellowed across Europe, but the cows were milked. On December 7, 1941, the Japanese attacked Pearl Harbor, but the cows were milked. In 1945, my seventeen-year-old father enlisted in the navy, but the cows were milked. Dien Bein Phu fell in 1954, Kennedy was assassinated in 1963, Nixon resigned in 1974, the Challenger exploded in 1986, and the Berlin Wall fell in 1989. And the cows were milked.

I remember one day in the early 1980s when the cows almost weren't milked. I woke from a sound sleep in the quiet darkness of my bedroom at 5:30 a.m. It was the same bedroom my father had slept in as a boy. I lay there, confused why I was awake. It was dark, it was quiet, and nothing stirred. What had wakened me? I got up and walked to my window. The farmyard was dark and silent. And then of a sudden I knew why I'd woken up. For the first time in my life at 5:30 in the morning the milking parlor was dark. Where was our foreman, Dean?

Alarmed, I called out, "Dad!" and from the master bedroom my father, awake and alert, replied, "I called Dean. His truck wouldn't start. But he's on his way now." Reassured, I went back to bed and instantly fell back into a deep sleep.

Other than starting thirty minutes late that one morning, the cows had been milked like clockwork for over a century. And that afternoon in 1996 as doctors worked to save Mike's life, my dad milked the cows.

It would be nice to say that my father was close to all of his children, but that's not the case. For reasons I've never fully understood, my dad and my older three brothers did not get along.

Mike is the reason I have some sense of the tension that existed between Adam, Eve, Cain, and Abel. Mike didn't like to be told what to do by a father he didn't respect, and neither did Cain. Adam probably came in for lunch some days and told Eve, "Hell, you'll never believe what that boy has done now!" So did Calvin. Abel probably got blamed because tools were left lying on the ground or because the calves were bawling with hunger. I did. Usually I could plead my innocence. Mike used those tools and the calves were Mike's to feed, but sometimes I was blamed for Mike's misdeeds. I didn't put a hole in the back window with my pellet gun, but I got blamed for it. And maybe Abel wasn't perfect and liked to run and tell his dad all the bad things that Cain was doing; I sure did.

In the mid 1990s, before Mike's accident, my dad's prostate cancer returned. On hearing the news, my brother Mike smiled and said to Dad, "I hope you die." Understandably then, things were tense between this father and son. And so, when Mike was airlifted to Salk Lake City, my father refused all our neighbors' offers of help, and stayed home to milk the cows. With Mike on a ventilator, our seventy-year-old father resumed his role as manager of the farm. I was an accountant then, so I stepped into help my father get a handle on the farm's books. Within a week, I discovered Mike had drawn $80,000 on the farm's line of credit without my dad's knowledge.

My father was devastated by Mike's theft, and suddenly, with Mike in intensive care and $80,000 of unexpected debt on the farm books, what happened in 1931 to Clarence seemed like it was going to happen again in 1996 to Calvin. Here it was —my worst nightmare, the fate I'd dreaded since the age of ten. The farm was on the brink of foreclosure.

Then the accountant in me realized that Mike had formed his own corporation and it was that entity that was in debt, not my dad's land or cows. I'm not proud of what I did next: I told my dad to let Mike go bankrupt. Mike hated Dad, Mike hated me, and this was Mike's problem. I advised Dad to walk away. Dad looked at me with disappointment in his eyes and explained, "Matthew, the bank gave Mike that money because he is my son—they loaned Mike that money because they knew I'd be good for it. I can't forsake that debt."

Mike wished Dad dead, stole his money and hocked his farm, but Calvin was going to pay his son's debts in full. There was only one option to come up with that kind of money, pay Mike's debts, and save the land. The cows would have to be sold.

Three weeks later, with Mike still in the hospital with a shattered pelvis, Dad sold the herd.

An obtuse but well-meaning neighbor was visiting Mike in the intensive care unit and let slip the news that the cows were gone. Mike was crushed—we'd kept the knowledge of the cattle sale from him out of fear for his health, and this development absolutely blindsided him. Four weeks prior to this, Mike's second marriage ended in the wreckage of his rage. His soon-to-be ex-wife had taken her children and fled. A week after that, Mike and his motorcycle lay crushed under a car in the middle of an intersection, and now he learned that his theft had cost him his livelihood. He lay in his hospital bed, tethered to machines and wept.

Dad never made the two-hour trip to Mike's hospital bed, even after the cows were sold and the milking parlor was dark. Dad and Mike never spoke again.

There is one final sheet of paper in my dresser. It's a deed dated 2012. It transferred the last remaining fifty acres of the farm from my father's irrevocable trust to me, his youngest son. A few months before he died in 2002, Dad took me to the lawyer's office.

"Matthew," he said, "drive me down to the attorney's office, we've got some paperwork to do."

When we were sitting in front of the lawyer, Dad asked Mr. Hoggan to draw up papers transferring all four hundred and thirty acres to me. I was shocked—I had no idea he was contemplating this. My greatest wish had come true. The farm was mine. I opened my mouth to say yes, and said, "No."

I couldn't believe what I was doing. I actually said no. It was my father's turn to be shocked.

I didn't want the farm that way. My siblings would hate me if I let them be disinherited. So, I said no. It turns out Dad didn't even tell Mom that he intended to give me their home.

It turns out it didn't matter. Soon after, my parents passed away. By the time the farm was divided up and split between us ten years later, only one of my siblings was still speaking to me. I gave up the lion's share of the family farm for family peace, and I and lost both. Most of my siblings wanted the homestead, too, but Dad was firm on that point: the homestead was to be mine. They could take the lower ground, but not the farmyard, not Clarence's house, not Grace's trees, not the waterfall.

Today, I'm still close to one sibling, a sister, Francine. She's the only sibling who forgave my father for giving me the homestead. She lives on the East Coast now, but a couple of times a year she comes to visit me, see old friends, and walk amongst the roses and honeysuckle.

Giving my father's eulogy, my sister Marianne said, "Our father had six children: Marianne, Jordan, Francine, Mike and Steven, and later, to his lasting delight, Matthew." She spoke the truth and I should know: I'm Matthew. I grew up in the warm rays of my parents' love, but I know what it's like to work in the field next to jealous brothers who would have liked nothing more than to strangle their little brother.

There is so much more I wish I knew about my father, so much I'd like to ask him. I was thirty-two years old when my parents died. I thought I knew everything when I was young. I wish that were true. In the months before he died, my father recorded dozens of hours of cassette tapes with his life history. Stories about growing up on the family farm. About his pony, Spot. About plowing fields all day with teams of horses. About the family's first tractor. About enlisting in the Navy to fight the Japanese. About serving as a lieutenant in the Army during the Korean War. About courting and marrying a pretty, young nurse who was caring for my grandfather LeRoy after he suffered a heart attack. About saving Mrs. Webb's life that day her baby was born. About being a farmer.

But when we tried to play those tapes, we discovered that

something had gone wrong; maybe Dad pushed the wrong button. Nothing had recorded.

I have four daughters, and they're best friends. But sometimes I wonder if the farm will tear them apart as it tore apart the four generations that preceded them. In The Book of Numbers, Moses recorded, "The Lord is longsuffering, and of great mercy, forgiving iniquity and transgression, [but] visiting the iniquity of the fathers upon the children unto the third and fourth generation."

I hope that the sins of their fathers will not be visited upon them, and that for a time, at least, the serpent sleeps. Perhaps, in the words of Ecclesiastes, it's "a time to heal...a time of peace."

19

The Campout

Jef Huntsman

Breathtaking hikes across bubbling mountain streams
Impetuous acres of wildflowers color the hills
Kiss of sunshine, warm, soft, and perfumed.
A deer turns and scampers away.
Stomachs delight over campfire beans and charred dogs.
Wild open spaces, fresh mountain air, glowing sunset
Then night falls,

Thumps of hail shred the forest
like notes blasted from an AC/DC concert
Riveting off the thin fabric of our new Walmart tent.
We huddle in owl-eyed worrisome cuddle.
The sagging roof clamps to claustrophobic containment.
The pounding hail nods to its friend—screaming rain.
At first heady drips, then flowing like millions of clear
    kite strings.
The splashes of mud puddles forming and distant frogs
    croaking.

Tent billows and contracts while wind howls through
     the darkness.
Our peaceful camping eve in the hands of horror and
     bellow.
I pull the zipper of our bags tighter to our necks.
Breath thick, frozen. Eyes wide, the color of bone dust.
Rumbles and booms scamper like wild horses storming
     by.
Faint shadows of whipped trees dance to the uproar.
Rivers in cold streams wobble like snakes down the tent.
Like the boy with the finger in the dam, I press the
     fabric.
The current surges chilling the hair to attention.
More leaks, more puddles form across our bedding.
Rippling down backpacks, plunking on a Coleman
     lantern.
Wetness thick enough to taste. Panic tightens, fingers
     clench.
We quickly sit up and scoot, centering, in an island.
Hopeful refuge without our visitor's sodden shadow.
Lightning wallops the ground, the cloth lights in a flash
Outlining streaked appendages in blackened silhouette.
Frito bag floats by, bunches against the flotsam in the
     corner.
Blackish liquid soaks our clothes and ripples our worn
     faces.
Lovers in a swamp of drenched supplies and lost
     dreams
Wait, shivering until a morning sun might grace with
     relief.
Then daybreak beckons,

Exhaustion peers through unzipped flaps and tendril
    streams.
The clouds have been scattered away by the warming
    beast
Whose rays stream in like fingers calling us forward.
Silently, we follow the muddy path to our car
Which beeps a sodden welcome at our approach.
Motor roars, wipers toss away remnants of last night.
We hunch down towards the heater vents—hoping,
driving fast with gladdened smiles and trembling
    chuckles.
Leaving the tent, cooler, soggy bread, and lantern to
those fools seeking the daydream of solitude and peace.

20

My Family Tree

Lorin Grace

HIGH IN THE UINTA MOUNTAINS, along a rough, narrow-paved road, is a perfect camping spot for the weekend explorer and the social media environmentalist. The grassy meadow surrounded by tall pines has it all: easy access, gentle hikes, and a mountain full of quaking aspen. And no bathrooms or running water, conveniences many people will forgo for a weekend in a quest to get back to nature. I know this because it had been my family's camping spot since 1927, long before the land was part of the national forest.

Each year someone new discovers this idyllic spot and claims it as their own. Though not an official camping spot, the US Forest Service allows camping there as long as users practice the Leave no Trace principles. Yet is isn't hard to find the place where fires have burned to cook s'mores for other campers. In late summer months at the far end of the meadow, sheepherder's trailers take up residence, still allowing plenty of room for those who wish to commune with nature to camp.

After setting up camp, most people don't wait long before

pulling out their cameras to take selfies and Instagram worthy nature pictures. For the remote spot was blessed with an extra dose of beauty.

One of the popular hikes out of the meadow is up a wide trail leading southward into the trees covering the quaking aspen-covered knoll. Even the most inexperienced day hikers have no problem climbing the gentle rise of the hill. There they look over a grove of Utah's state tree. School children will tell their parents how in 2014 the state tree was officially changed to the "quakies" because the colony of trees grows out of the same root system, representing how, by working together, Utahns can reach new heights. Someone may tell their fellow hikers that the largest living organism in the world is a group of 47,000 Aspen near Richfield, Utah named Pando. The armchair environmentalist in the group will point out Pando is slowly dying due in part to human encroachment. Eventually, someone will notice the unnatural scars on the trees. Letters and numbers, dates and names mark many of the largest trees.

Some hikers will look over the woods they can view from the top of the knoll and talk about the terrible people who marred the trees. The hopeless romantic may be brave enough to point to initials inside of hearts and wonder aloud if love lasted as long as the tree. Others, cursing those who abused the trees, will continue to walk up the old wide trail to find trees unmarred by previous hikers. They will look down on other fertile basins and rejoice in a land untouched by man (as if such a place exists).

None of them see what I see when I stand in the same place. The fertile valley south of the meadow was once called Blue Lake. But when the road which gave them access to their camping spot was put in years ago, the lake dried up and disappeared along with the natural spring of cool, clear water. Over the ridge where the tall pines grow, they may not recognize lodgepole pine. They only see the forest, not the trees. Focus on the scars and not the names. And they cannot appreciate a lake no longer there or history they've never heard.

I was always afraid to get too close to the lake. My grandma nearly drowned in Blue Lake, the one that isn't there. Her story has been handed down for more than half a century by those who remember the water there and drank from the spring. The lake my father swam in with his cousins. The lake I was too scared to even wade in. The lake, like many things about the area only, lives in old photographs and fading memories.

When I visit the high mountain meadow, I recall family photographs from the 40s and 50s tucked into old albums. Photos of the Johnson Sawmill, known to us as Wolf Creek.

From 1927 to 1954, a sawmill run by a father and his five sons occupied the area, turning trees into lumber which helped to build houses and towns across the state. A sawmill that taught their sons and daughters the value of hard work and the value of family.

The lodgepole pines over the ridge have a special meaning for me. For years, like my father before me, I slept in a bed made of one of those trees. Trees cut down and milled by my grandfather then lovingly crafted. Both of my sons have used the bed since. . Leftover lumber from those trees made the cradle my children first slept in when they were born. Few people can trace the lumber used to make their furniture to the spot of ground it grew on. The old family sawmill was dismantled and removed long before I was born, but I know where to find its remains. I know the wonderful, wide hiking trail was once the end of a logging road where horses and later trucks brought felled trees down to the mill.

The weekend hikers don't realize that for over a quarter of a century the "untouched" land was judiciously harvested. Perhaps furniture or beams in the hikers' grandparents' homes came from the mountain surrounding the campground they now enjoy. They don't see the old moonshine still discovered and destroyed by my great-grandfather. Or the miles of pipe laid by him and his sons to bring water to the small towns of Hanna and Tabiona, possibly at my great-grandfather's expense. The hikers don't know that for a brief period between being no-man's-land and the government's land, that part of the mountain was Johnson land.

Today, the Johnsons have no legal claim to the federally owned land, yet in memories and heart, the meadow and surrounding hill still belong to the family. We bring our children there to discover the wonders of the wilderness and to later appreciate the joys of indoor plumbing. Around the campfire, conditions permitting, or battery powered lanterns, we tell stories of grandfathers, great-aunts and uncles, some living and many passed. Stories which tie us together, united by invisible ties, just as the grove of quaking aspen are liked by their roots. By day, we take them to the grove and point out names and dates. Kenny '52 and Linda in '76, the best we can we identify each name. Most of the carved names are grouped by family. My name appears twice, once under my father and again with my husband and children. Both times carefully added to older trees, so the cuts were not too deep.

What hikers don't realize when they study the scars marring the white bark is that they are looking at the living Johnson family tree.

21

The Willow

Isaac Timm

Planted to grow quickly,
to block the wind,
shade the young garden,
the three sisters who spun
turned rough prairie skirts
into magnolias.

In 1878 lightning split it,
blasting both sides to the ground
but the rancher let it grow
new shoots formed fingers,
then arms stretching
from the rails of broken
trunk, sinews growing over
reunions, church
gatherings, weddings.

It lives, it dies, but always

reborn, spreading, leaving behind
blackened scars, smooth caverns
of heartwood where earth can be heard.

Both sides of the green-open embrace
can be climbed, follow bark smoothed by hands,
decade after decade,
up into the canopy of green among
fluted leaves to look down on the girls
in their Sunday dresses
who spin and spin and spin.

22

Walking into Home
Star Coulbrooke

WE STOP at the bottom of Big Hollow to listen to the shush of wind through a lone red cedar, also known as Rocky Mountain Juniper. Its soft flat needle edges sway in clusters on a twenty-foot spread of thick branches that stretch over a cushion of rich brown loam. Hundreds of cedar/junipers crowd the surrounding hills and hollows.

We've known this place all our lives. Big Hollow is part of a 160-acre parcel of land in Riverdale, Idaho, granted for home-steading to our grandfather on November 13, 1884. Dad, the youngest of eleven children, purchased the homestead from his widowed mother January 27, 1941, for "$1.00 and natural love and affection." Mother sold it to LeeAnn, her youngest, on April 25, 1978, when she remarried and moved to St. George, Utah.

LeeAnn and I have walked in the southeast Idaho moun-tains every weekend since 1994, when Mother came back to Riverdale after her husband died. This is how we get away from it all, by coming back to the place that gives us a sense of purpose, a sense of who we are, of where we fit in the natural landscape.

Skirting the foot of Big Hollow, we find pinkies blooming on the rocky slopes. Not spring beauties, the fragile pink and white blooms we find after the first snowmelt gives way to snowdrops or Indian parsnip, as those tiny white ice-cluster flowers are known in other locales. These plants our family always called pinkies are low growing and hardy with dark green dandelion-like foliage and fuchsia-colored blossoms only an eighth inch wide. We found their name in one of the western weed and flower guides we pore over periodically, but we've forgotten it. The names we use for what surrounds us in these homeland hills are as personal and vital as our own. Pinkies will always be pinkies to us, cedars always cedars, however they've been labeled elsewhere.

A hawk drifts in the blue air high above Cedar Hollow, where a few deer stand watching us make our way up the hillside to the canal road. It's dry for the end of March, and the deer have already shed their gray winter coats for the sleek golden camouflage of summer. Every season asks us to adapt. We add or shed layers along with the deer and coyotes. We pay attention to the migration of songbirds, of ducks and geese, of wild turkeys. We know they move, not to calendar-time, but to subtle changes we can't discern and may never understand.

Changes we do understand are coming to Riverdale. People have seen the rolling hills and lush river valley, and they want to live here. We don't blame them. And we don't blame our neighbors, most of whom are cousins, for choosing to sell their burden of land that has kept them struggling to make ends meet. We ponder what our responsibility will be to these new neighbors who take root like colorful weeds. Perhaps they will grow on us in positive ways, with names that become part of the local fabric, like pinkies. Like some of our favorite wild-flowers.

Every spring we look for the first bluebell, the first johnny jump-up (Nuttall violet), the first cowslip, also known as glacier lilies. Buttercups (yellowbell or yellow fritillary) usually come before any of these, but they are rare, their upside-down, deep-cupped blossom short-lived. I thought my time on the family farm would be short-lived. It took leaving for a few years and coming back before I could appreciate this legacy from our pioneering ancestors.

I had thought the big city suited me better. Not so for LeeAnn. She has always revered the family farm and the wild and tame animals that live here. When Dad died in 1962, she talked Mother into keeping the place. It took some doing, but Mother managed. She found a job in town, sold the cows, and leased the fields. When she remarried sixteen years later and moved to southern Utah, she offered to sell the farm to LeeAnn and her husband, Clyde. They made the last payment on it shortly after Mother died in 1999, and fallowed the fields for wildlife habitat.

On our way back down the hill, we look out over the valley and rolling hillsides nestled in the blue of distant mountains, and we forgive the ever-increasing number of houses that interrupt our view. After all, our grandfather built here too, and so did his children. It wouldn't be home without the people, the community. Like it or not, the landscape changes, and it shouldn't matter who was here first, as long as we take care of each other. We're all weeds, all out of place, no matter how long it has been since we arrived.

Maybe that's where we fit. In our longing for home, we've forgotten we're only visitors, and what we're walking away from is fear of our own erasure from the landscape. For hundreds of years before the Bear River Massacre of 1863, the place we call Riverdale was dotted with the tepees of Shoshone and Bannock Indians. Almost every shred of evidence that they ever existed has been lifted from the soil. We too are destined to lose the land and lifestyle we know and love, and so we love it as it evolves, weeds and all.

We've come to the prickly pear knoll at the edge of Maple Hollow, a short walk down the hill to the old garden plot behind the farmhouse. We're careful where we set our feet, avoiding prickly pear spines and remembering the four baby cottontails we almost stepped on last spring. Startled, they hop-scurried through an opening in the dry grass that curved against a stand of sagebrush and disappeared. But I see them in my mind, where I carry the memories of landscape, the history of family, the names of plants. And I recognize my place, my obligation to the land and all who live here, as I'm walking into home.

23

Trophy

Brock Dethier

We thrash to the summit.
Harsh snow squalls obscure the view.
Gusts snap our jackets.

Your mittens fail against windblown pellets
and even an hour's steep climb
doesn't warm me.

We spot early season paintbrush,
molting elk trotting the facing slope
in a patch of mid-flurry sun,

when Steersheads! you cry.
Snowmelt flower, low, rare,
easily missed,

perfectly named for its shape,
bone white streaked
with roof-of-the-mouth pink.

Cold, we scramble down,
content to have captured
the curve of its horns.

24

Old Timer

Tim Keller

I WAS slow getting into position. Clouds of frozen breath billowed around me like exhaust from a steam engine. This was the first opening day in years we'd had snow, and what a storm it had been. None of us were prepared for it. I had to cut across a promising draw to make up for lost time. Still, I was behind.

By the time I crested the ridgeline, the sun shone brilliant white on the bluffs below, illuminating even the shadows. High on the mountain top, I stopped to catch my breath. The freezing air smelled of pine and mountain sage. The sound of the river, more than a mile below, welcomed me back.

The scolding of distant magpies caught my attention. They dipped and circled as if to say, "This way, slowpoke. Over here."

A shot rang out. Then two, then more. A line of bouncing white butts crossing the next ridge over told the tale. The deer had spooked too soon, and too far away to shoot. Not that the boys didn't try. I didn't even un-shoulder my rifle. I couldn't suppress a smile, though.

I thought about telling them. Their low man had been out of

position by as much as a football field and the others had sky-lined too soon—then there was the noise, everyone yelling to everyone else—and all had ignored the magpies. But my nephews are adults now, men accomplished in their own right with families of their own. Correcting them unbidden felt presumptuous.

My nephew Jacob's thirteen-year-old son Elliot's voice rang out as he approached. "I have a cactus in my leg." Elliot gesticulated wildly at the offending appendage. "Literally—in my leg!"

How far had he duck-walked with a prickly-pear embedded in his thigh just to show us, or for that matter what he expected upon arrival, was anyone's guess. That he intended indictment was clear, but of whom and for what remained unclear. His father gazed in the boy's direction and snorted.

I caught a glimpse of my father in Jacob's eyes just then and definitely heard him in Jacob's voice when he said, "Well, pull it out, then."

I stifled a laugh. Jacob was the only one of his generation old enough to have really hunted with Dad, and it showed. My father's influence and Jacob's Marine Corps training precluded any chance of a sympathetic response.

————

It happens every September: the air's first chill. Green morphs to yellows and vibrant reds. Flocks of geese fly high in V formations, headed south for the winter. My awareness almost imperceptibly heightens, and I begin scanning the mountain slopes in anticipation of crisp October mornings when I'll be awake before the sun, hauling my butt to places I no longer have any business being.

I'm fortunate to have spent most of my autumns this way.

Autumn is the best season to be in the mountains. Of course I know that's subjective. The skier/boarder crowd, for instance, obviously prefer the deep freeze and powdery snow drifts of winter.

Others relish the rebirth of wild flowers and leaves and the return of migratory fauna that come with Spring. And many if not most prefer to crowd the heights to escape the summer heat and revel in the bounties of summer's abundance.

And that's great, all of it; for me, though, nothing compares to the vivid colors and cooler days of fall, when the insects, and the tourists, have gone. An almost preternatural calm presides, as though mountains themselves are already asleep, abandoned, or at least in the process of becoming so, like a soon-to-be ghost town. But not—the breath of winter can be felt in blizzards of red and yellow leaves. And the summer's bounty has ensured creatures great and small are in their best condition of the year: the perfect time to hunt.

Hunting embodies a certain grace, an homage to a time of necessity. Hunting is also great sport. Our quarry have the strength, the speed, and an enormous sensory advantage and have adapted to and know the terrain.

Our human advantages are but equalizers. Weaponry being the most obvious, but all our advantages stem from intellect. We outsmart our quarry (sometimes). And yet, more times than not, we come home empty-handed.

When I was a kid, taking a buck meant bragging rights. But it was always framed in terms of harvest, of respect for the game, and gratitude for the life we took. A moment of respect for the fallen, an expression of gratitude for its life, and of course, for the sustenance the meat provides. Though to be honest, much of it seemed perfunctory, like saying grace before the family meal. We were indeed grateful, but grace or not, the food was prepared and ready to eat: a reality unalterable by a nicety. Only later, as an adult, did I begin to appreciate these rituals.

———

It's too easy I think, to chalk up Elliot's behavior as an exemplar of his generation or environment. True, he was young, and had recently moved to Idaho from California. He had yet to acclimate. And hunting had likely been pitched to him by family and new friends alike as fun and adventurous, educational even. But the capacity to appreciate, if not commune with nature, comes at a price.

Near the top of Devil's Hill, where the grade is steep, the rocks are sharp, and even the plant life is hostile, the fire in his sea-level lungs (not to mention his thigh) won out. Elliot didn't fully understand himself why he was there. Without the drive, the need, or connection to the land, hunting was just too hard. I made room for the possibility that he would acquire an appreciation for it, if only for his father's sake, but that wouldn't come anytime soon.

The following morning, he elected to stay home. His cousins evidently felt similarly.

I understood well their point of view.

———

As a kid, I hunted out of expectation from peers and family alike. It was what boys did. Under the scrutiny and tutelage of men like my father, I and the boys I grew up with came into our own. On the mountain, we were men. Journeymen perhaps, but men all the same with responsibilities to the group effort.

I was eight the first time my father took me hunting. He's

been gone seven years now and it's been some forty since I heard him say, without slowing his horse, "Grab the tail, hold't." *Meaning, we're late and out of position, grab the horse's tail, dodge the inevitable kicks, and hold on no matter how many rocks and trees it drags you over. And whatever you do, don't tell your mother.*

Indeed, I once got lost. Dad and his cousin Bud dropped me on a high bluff and galloped off after some deer they'd spotted. I was to "Stay right here," but they were gone a long time. Forever, really. Long enough for me to consider I was on a mountaintop in the middle of a forest where creatures like mountain lions, coyotes, or bears might come looking for a snack. Besides, I had a pretty good idea where they'd gone.

Except I didn't.

As I entered the trees below, I lost all sense of direction and did the only thing I could think of: walk downhill and pray. Eventually, I spied a truck in the distance and made a beeline for it. Imagine my surprise to find it was our truck. The doors were locked, so I crawled into the bed and slept until Dad made his way back at dusk to go for help.

I worried I'd be in trouble for leaving. But instead I was praised for my resourcefulness. There at the truck, and at home in front of my mom (who wasn't fooled for second) and everyone. Sadly—rather than *help* dad bring down the deer he'd abandoned to search for me—I had to go to school the next day. Unfair as that seemed, the whole experience ended far better than we had any right to expect.

———

By the time I was old enough to actually hunt, Dad seemed hopelessly out of touch. As a newly minted teenager, I questioned everything. Forged from the same metal but by vastly different forces, mine and my father's views of the world, politics and philosophy, already hopelessly divergent, were getting worse. By age fourteen, I was openly pointing out the disparity between science and the teachings of our church.

———

Dad stopped to rest his horse near the summit of some nameless mountain. We'd hunted hard all the way to the top to no avail. And I was one hundred percent ready to be done, an opinion I voiced in a way that I'm sure sounded bratty.

"There ain't no deer up here," I said.

Dad grinned. "No easy ones anyway."

He had a million of those. Scandinavia's answer to Confucius, my Dad; complete with fortune-cookie delivery. Like another old chestnut: *They're where you find them.* Or my favorite, *if they aren't where you are, you gotta go where you aren't.* But I digress.

"But if you don't want one," Dad drawled. "There's plenty to do at home."

Bratty I was, but not so stupid that I didn't know a test when I heard one. But a test of what? Endurance, temperament, skill? Whatever it was, I was in no mood.

I hadn't even seen a track and hardly needed to be Jim Bridger to know that deer leave them. No tracks, no deer. It was a pretty simple equation.

"Well?" he snapped.

No hint of drawl this time.

"Fine!" I huffed. "What do you want me to do?"

Dad took me by the shoulders and turned until I was looking just where he wanted. "See that saddle down there?"

I nodded, though it was all I could do not to groan. The saddle in question was several hundred yards below. The climb down met another one back up.

"Head for that saddle but don't cross it until you're even with that big cedar." I hated directions like that. *It's a forest, Dad! Maybe you could be more specific?*

Thankfully, this time at least, there actually was a cedar in the direction he pointed and a large one at that. I took a step to begin the hike but was pulled back.

"Once you cross over," added my dad, "walk 400 steps, then circle back. That's 400—you count em. No more, no less. Understand?"

I stifled an eye roll and nodded.

"And pay attention," he called after me. "Whatever happens will happen fast."

I waved my understanding.

Exactly 400 steps from the crest above the aforementioned cedar, two big bucks leapt from their beds. I worked my slide action .3006 like a demented trombonist until the empty rifle clicked. There wasn't time for anything else. When the dust cleared, the largest buck I'd ever taken lay at my feet.

Somewhere between my shouts of, "I got him, I got him," Dad's rifle took the other.

"You don't just storm up a mountain like the beach at Normandy," Dad explained as I dutifully field-dressed our prizes. "Oh, you might get lucky, happen on a doe or a little one that way, but the big ones will always be gone. Make a plan, sacrifice the least-likely area, get in position, and then hunt."

That nugget of wisdom, like so many others, applied to far more than hunting, and like so many others, were lessons that I never forgot.

By fifteen I was openly gay. We had little or nothing to say to each other, could barely make eye contact. When we spoke at all it was generally antagonistic.

But none of that mattered on the mountain. On the mountain I learned about life, the area, and our family's history with it.

I listened with rapt attention as he told of the Mink Creek Ghost. The time his father, then a nine-year-old boy, entrusted, along with his older brother with the family's herd of sheep, had walked alone from Mink Creek to Mantua for supplies: a sixty-three mile trip and back, in the winter, in the 1870s, by himself.

Dad could really weave a tale. It was on the mountain that he told of the fire at the old Yellow Schoolhouse. I can still hear him laugh as described girls crying, "Put it out, put it out," while he and the other boys chanted, "Let her burn. Let her burn."

Hard as it was to reconcile with the man I knew, I learned that Dad had been a hellion once himself. He even swore from time to time (provided ladies weren't present). His father, already an old man when Dad was born, had died when Dad was a teenager. After that, Dad just sort of went wild.

I'm pretty sure I was the first to hear about the time he'd shown up at a church dance drunk, a story which he always followed-up with the tale of tale of how he came to serve a Mormon mission; how early the following morning, hung-over and sick, he answered a pounding on the door.

"It was there on the enclosed front porch the old bishop called me on a mission!" Dad laughed. "A couple weeks later, I was in Georgia."

He'd been home only three weeks when he was drafted into the Korean War. The train from basic training to Seattle and the ship that would take him to deployment stopped in Montpelier, Idaho. Less than twenty miles from his home. "My buddies got off to stretch their legs. But I didn't dare. I could have walked home," he confided. "I so wanted to see my mom again." He cleared his throat. "But I stayed on the train."

———

By senior year I was strong enough and independent enough to hunt on my own, and had any number of successful hunts under my belt. I began to hunt with other people. I hunted with friends, both old and new and had a great time. I even guided my neighbor's teenage son to his first elk. We had just begun field dressing it when my father and older brother appeared on the plateau, a few hundred yards below. I watched as Dad lifted his binoculars, then put them away and rode off.

My partners were upset, but I just laughed. *Our elk, our responsibility.* That scene repeated itself the following year when I took a large bull of my own. Dad rode up on his horse, regarded me and my elk, then rode on. I wasn't laughing that time; it took two days to pack it out.

I hunted with a lot of different people back then. Dad was getting older and couldn't make it up as often, while I couldn't seem to keep away. Those trips were more for fun than anything else. More often than not, however, the end of the season would find me on Devil's Hill or The Steeps, dragging a deer down with my dad. I voiced this observation once.

Ever modest, he said, "Hunting is as much about understanding the competition as the deer themselves. If you understand what you're after, and those that'd keep you from it, well, you just about can't go wrong."

My breathing came in great gasping gulps, yet I fell behind with every step. I was in great shape, in my twenties, but no match for my brother's horse. Just like the previous week, he'd eventually be ahead by as much as a draw. Dad, having taken the low brush near the river, wouldn't know anything about it until it was all over. Due to my refusal to ride a horse, I knew Dad would only tell me to hurry faster—if I told him that is, which I wouldn't.

As they disappeared I got an idea. Instead of staying in position, I double-timed it over the summit to intercept them as they hunted back around.

Jacob followed suit and took a good buck as soon as we crossed, and in the doing, he jumped a much larger one.

I ran to a boulder to lean my borrowed .243 across, then fired and missed as the deer stotted away until finally, at extreme range and a mere jump from going over the ridge, it stopped and looked back to gloat. I fired. He collapsed and rolled into a ravine.

My father and brother arrived late on the scene, while I, the conquering hero, moved to collect my prize. The buck had chosen a most inconvenient final resting place, about halfway down the opposite side of a steep draw, in thick chaparral. Down I trudged, then fought my way back up through brush. When I grabbed his antlers, he stood up.

I squealed.

He bleated.

I uttered any number of forbidden words.

He ran over the top of me.

And the fight was on.

I rolled out of my fall and into shooting position just in time to hear my father yell, "Don't shoot!"

The deer was booking it away from the forest land to Mr. Johnson's well-posted and well-patrolled ranch. I was to "chase it down" and use my knife.

Given the ease with which he'd taken me down the first time, this seemed neither advisable nor even possible. But Dad had spoken.

Still, the buck was pulling away at such a pace that I deemed there to be no choice. I pulled up and fired. He crumpled. Dad went apoplectic, stomping, yelling, waving his arms like he was guiding an airplane into the terminal. Much noisier it seemed to me than my shot had been. Johnson had to have heard us by then.

Too focused on Dad to pay much attention to the trail ahead, I was stopped short by the blood-snorting buck now charging right at me. He was definitely having a bad day, and by all accounts, appeared determined to share it.

This time Dad yelled, "Shoot! Shoot! SHOOT!" Which freaked me out more than the deer. A blast to the neck slowed his charge but did little to affect its course. I racked the lever and pulled the trigger, *click*. I was out.

I drew my knife.

The buck closed.

We impacted like opposing linemen. A brief albeit intense struggle later... I conducted a hurried field dressing. Then Jacob and I raced down the mountain, buck in tow.

We heard Johnson's truck before it came into view, and we dove into a drainage, rolling the deer over the top of us for camouflage. As soon as the truck passed, we each grabbed an antler and sprinted down Johnson's driveway to the gate. Dad's truck appeared. We loaded the deer and sped off before Johnson could return.

"How'd you get around there so fast?" my brother asked.

"We didn't," said Jacob. "We went over the top and met you coming around."

I spied a glimmer of admiration in Dad's eyes.

———

Owing to a career move to the East Coast, it had been years since I'd hunted. A rare visit home found my father waking me at dawn for a hunt.

Dad could have taken the giant buck with ease. He was always the better shot. He chose instead to heckle me. "Missed," he said, stating the obvious at my first shot. "Ah, you didn't even scare him," at my second. I hurled off my pack and laid the rifle across it. The solid whump and a crumpling buck prompted a whoop from Dad, followed by, "nice shooting, smart move with that back pack."

Hunting transcended politics, religion, even sexuality. Everything I knew of Dad's youth and family history and most life lessons was passed down via Sermon on the Mount. It was on the mountain I learned that he was the baby of the family, "spoiled rotten," he chuckled. There was the time he dropped two deer with one bullet. That his brothers considered him, "the luckiest little shit in the territory."

"Only took me with cuz they knew they'd see deer."

I opined that luck repeated makes a pattern. He smiled.

———

Jacob took his son's desire to stay home in stride, suggesting that since the kids wouldn't be coming, we should go to The Steeps. Jake, his brother Jonathon, recently retired from the army, and my youngest nephew, Jade. Jacob and I had hunted together through most of his youth; Todd and I, the last several years.

I pulled off an old logging road next to a cattle guard. "Jonathon, head back down the road about seventy-five yards. Then swing up and around the face just above the tree line, and back to the truck like the hand of a clock.

To Jacob— "Wait ten minutes, then sneak off through those pines at a forty-five-degree angle."

"Jade—Head downhill until you find a deer trail; there'll be a lot of them, just pick one and go until you see the big rocks, then sit on one and wait till we call you back."

"What are you going to do?" Todd asked.

"Hang out and wait for a deer," I said.

He snorted. "Here—by the truck."

"Unless you shoot him first," I said. "Better get going."

Todd shook his head and took off.

"And pay attention," I called after him. "Whatever happens will happen fast."

He waved without turning.

Within minutes, Jonathon cut loose with a string of inarticulate bellows before pulling himself together. "Buck, big buck, 3 o'clock!" he shouted.

The message came a little late. The deer had bounded onto the road in front of me. My rifle was up, my finger already on the trigger. After a split second of eye contact, I lowered the gun, and he bounded down the mountain.

A shot, another, then Jade's shouts of, "I got him," rang out from below.

Jonathon joined me on the logging road. "He crossed right in front of you."

I nodded.

"How'd you know?"

"An old buck will only break as a last resort," I said. "Often as not they'll try and double back between drivers. And deer are just like people in that they'd rather go easy than hard. Leaving a blocker on the road just made sense."

"Except you were too slow." He laughed.

I chuckled. "Yup," I said. "Too slow."

"So how do we find Jade?"

"Well, Todd got him, and those are his tracks; follow the buck's trail, he'll lead you to right to him."

I smiled as Jonathon leapt a deadfall and dropped at least fifteen feet onto the trail. I don't leap many deadfalls any more. And the mountains get a little steeper each year. But I'm not ready to give up my annual ritual, not yet, not ever—so long as I have anything to say about it. Every tree, stream, bush or boulder reminds me of some adventure or the occasional sermon. These days it is not as important for me to harvest a buck as it is just to be there, in its domain, matching wits.

By the time I'd worked my way around, they were washing their hands in the snow. I grabbed an antler and struggled with the buck until the boys took over, hauling it back up the mountainside faster than I could follow. As my nephews are eager to remind me, I'm the old-timer now.

25

Desert Mustang

Jeff Bateman

To run is to live, sage slaps at his knees,
alone with the kiss of a warm, desert breeze.

Alert in the silent, desolate space,
untouched by man, a state of grace.

Competing for fodder, water and space,
too many horses for this harsh place.

Hammering, chopping the dry desert air;
it swoops down low, driving them—where?

Instinct against them, they move as one,
white-eyed panic, onward they run.

Corralled, crowded, they strike out in fear.
Surrounded by steel, freedom so near.

Flat hand to muzzle, a tentative touch,
a start towards trust, it means so much.

Skin quivering under the path of my hand,
afraid but not bolting, now part of our band.

Halters and lead ropes, lariats, spurs,
patient progression, steady nerves.

First saddle, first bridle, first weight on his back,
no bucking, no kicking with each piece of tack.

Hundred-day champion, put to the test,
he proved his mettle, became the best.

Friend and companion, trust built two ways,
alone but together the rest of our days.

First printed in *Volatile When Mixed.*

26

Crossing Over

Stephen Page

ONCE THERE WAS A THIN, widowed, retired man named Jonathan who lived in a small cabin in the middle of a large patch of woods. Jonathan was sixty-two, but he was in excellent health. He had vibrant cheeks that beamed from under his clear blue eyes and shiny silver locks that hung low upon his forehead.

One fine summer day, Jonathan decided it was time he went on an adventure. He thought and remembered there was a beach some fifty miles east, one with yellow sand and a periwinkle sea. He used to take his wife there. Now, somehow, that the place seemed like a dream, like someone else's memory, a parallel universe. Maybe it never existed. He had to go there to see if it was real. But, he had no vehicle—no car, no pickup, no motorcycle, not even a bicycle. Many years ago, he decided he would not need one. He would have to walk. That would be no problem for Jonathan; he had been walking daily to the grocer's for years. It was only a two-hour jaunt, and he really did not want to go anywhere else since his wife died. He spent most of his time alone, reading in his cabin or sitting on his porch admiring the diversity of trees and listening to the multifarious song birds.

Books were Jonathan's favorite amusement. He loved to read. He always had. Some of his first memories were of reading books. Now, more than any other time in his life, since he missed his wife's companionship, he read incessantly. He read at breakfast, he read at noon, he read at night. Books were his life.

Realizing that he had not journeyed out of his cabin except to the grocer's for years, Jonathan decided it was undeniably time he went on an adventure. It would be a notable adventure, one that would be worthy of writing about. One that would someday become a book. One last great journey.

He opened his leather backpack and set it on the kitchen table. He would pack what he needed for a long trip. He opened his cupboards and fridge, studied the canned soups, the coffee, the bread, meat, cheese, fruit, soda cans, and bottles brimming with water. He shook his head. He removed from his bookshelf *The Odyssey, Sir Gawain and the Green Knight, Don Quixote, The Canterbury Tales, The Adventures of Huckleberry Finn, Call of the Wild, Into the Wild, Even Cowgirls Get the Blues, Tao: The Watercourse Way, The Underground Railroad,* and *The Trail of Tears.* He neatly stacked them sideways inside the pack so that the largest one would be flat against his back and the corners would not dig into his skin. He left his beloved copy of *Moby Dick* on his study desk only because the pack was now full, swung the pack onto his back, and slipped his arms into the straps. The pack weighed heavy upon his shoulders. He went to the front door, took his walking stick, and stepped outside.

He nimbly trod the path that led from his porch to the edge of the woods then opened to the dirt road that ran by the woods.

He lightly stepped and skipped along the dirt road heading east, kept to the road it as it ran through an expanse of cultivated wheat, then passed through a ridgeline of mountains.

He had not walked even half a mile past the ridgeline into a field of wild grasses when he felt an internal change beginning to take place. There was tightness in his jaw and in the upper part of his cheeks, a tingling sensation in his scalp, a clearing of his lungs, and a feeling that he was returning home. His original home.

After he had plodded along the dirt road for quite some time, his only companions a light plume of trailing dust and his short shadow, he heard a woman laughing. He stopped. The laughter continued. It was a trilling laughter accentuated in short, loud bursts that came from the other side of a hill in front of him. A Model-A Ford appeared over the hill. The raucous rattle of the engine muffled the woman's laughter. A Model-A Ford! Model-As hadn't been made in over a hundred years. The car bore down upon the spot where Jonathan was standing like he wasn't even there. The man in the driver's seat strained forward, wearing aviator goggles, a leather cap, and leather gloves. He had both hands firmly gripped on top of the steering wheel. The laughing woman in the passenger side wore a green dress and a floral scarf and with one hand held down a wide-brimmed hat upon her head. Jonathan leapt to the side of the road.

Neither the man nor the woman glanced in his direction as they barreled past, and Jonathan stepped back onto the road and stood in their dust cloud and studied them as they traveled in the direction from which he came. The woman's scarf fluttered behind her in the wind. The car became smaller and smaller as it distanced itself from Jonathan, and long after the sound of the engine faded, Jonathan could still hear the woman laughing—but, that too eventually abated, and the car became a speck then vanished. He turned and continued on his great adventure.

After trudging and dragging his feet for a number of uneventful hours, he came to a crossroad. It was a small two-lane paved road with a thin white center line and no shoulders. He checked traffic in both directions and saw no cars. Neither were there any houses near the road, only small green hills and fields of waxy lemon trees on the other side of the road. He strode across the road and halted on the other side.

The dirt road did not continue. He looked left and right, then behind him at the distant ridgeline. Everything was a bit hazy and out of focus. He studied the dust on his shoes then searched the ground. His shadow, now having lengthened, was stretching east. It made him look much taller than he was. He smiled. He watched his shadow and moved his arms up and down. Then he gripped his walking stick by the top handle, pointed it out in front of him, sliced the air with quick slashing strokes, parried with his shadow, stabbed it, chased it, then slipped the stick into a make-shift scabbard he created by forming the fingers and thumb of his left hand into an O-ring against his left hip.

He looked west. The sun was a scoop of orange sherbet melting upon the mountains, the light was diminishing, and the air was beginning to chill. Mosquitoes rose and the smell of lemons carried upon the dampening air.

Jonathan drew the sword from its scabbard in a sweeping motion, then lifted it above him and pointed it toward the crepuscular sky. He shouted triumphantly. An echo came back to him from the green hills.

The books felt good pressed against his back.

27

Safe Passage on Green River

Jo Lynne Harline

Sunlight splashes the rim of canyon walls
and standing rocks, and warms the sandbar
where we emerge from bedrolls to take down
tents, and repack our gear; we launch

the rafts and drift off in high spirits down
a serene stretch of cocoa-brown river
past banks of tamarisk and willow.
A boulder with black varnish demands our

attention like a billboard: ancient Fremont
petroglyphs depicting a parade or ceremonial
procession with warriors and flute-players.
We seem small below high, echoing walls.

A turkey vulture soars above, inspecting us.
Each of us has a mantra or a prayer for safe
passage paddling through wild rapids ahead;
we toss ritual offerings overboard (apples,

sunglasses, whatever) to appease the restless
river spirit a few minutes before our rafts go
plunging into fierce, foaming, thrashing waves.
I feel an insane, familiar adrenaline surge, then--

for this moment we are weightless, nothing
more than driftwood buoyed by swollen
currents, no more than pebbles polished by
grit and interminable churning waters.

28

Ah, Wilderness

HUMANS, HAWKS, AND ENVIRONMENTAL CORRECTNESS ON THE MUDDY RIO GRANDE

Dinty W. Moore

"You CAN STEER, CAN'T YOU?"

The question comes from Annie, a wiry, energetic woman of about fifty, with graying hair, dark eyes, a craggy face that belies countless hours under the sun. She wears Teva water shoes, neoprene bike shorts, black rowing gloves. I am here to relax, but Annie is all business.

"Well, can you?"

Thirteen of us — three guides and ten paying customers — stand on the Texas side of the Rio Grande, just east of Big Bend National Park, about to launch eight canoes. The canoes sit low in the water, laden with tents, poles, food, paddles, pots, pans, stoves, water jugs, and a cumbrous portable toilet we will come to call "The Groaner."

In their wisdom, the guides have paired Annie and me together, but having sized me up in my old tennis sneakers, cheap t-shirt, and denim shorts, she seems not so sure. Steering a canoe is a dicey prospect under any circumstance, given the vagaries of water and wind; but in whitewater, steering can be life or death. Annie has reason to be cautious.

"You do have a draw stroke, right?" She is sensing my hesitation. "You *do* know how to read water?"

The simple answer is "yes," but the Rio Grande is capricious; a swirling mess of brown river, fast-moving and sided by high canyon and undercut rock. I *do* know a bit about steering a canoe, though not enough that Annie's aggressive questioning doesn't immediately make me forget it all.

The pairing remains, because the guides don't want to hear dissent. Worse yet, from Annie's perspective, I am awarded the stern, where the course is set and corrections made. The canoe's rear seat falls to me not because of gender or expertise, but because I outweigh Annie dramatically.

She reluctantly takes the bow, and one by one, the guides push the eight canoes into the swift current. When it is our turn, Annie commences paddling, paddling with immense effort, paddling at a rate easily three-times more vigorous than the bow paddler in any of the other tandem boats. She paddles as if her very life depends on it, as if I have already announced loudly my plans to steer the canoe into the first dangerous hole I can find.

The evening before, thirteen of us meet in a motel in Odessa, Texas, home of the world's largest jackrabbit statue. We spend the following morning squeezed into a long blue Nantahala Outdoor Center van, riding across the endless flatness of the Permian Basin, all oil fields and bone-dry ranches. We drop down through Fort Stockton, Marathon, past the Tinaja Mountains, before we find the unmarked road to our river put-in, at Heath Canyon Ranch.

Aside from Annie, the guests on this trip include a pair of retired Vermont schoolteachers; a Bermuda physician named Thomas and his birdwatching British wife, Lu; Fiona, a young pharmaceutical saleswoman; two other doctors, both traveling solo; Bill, a retired engineer; and me. Both of the American doctors are named Dave, and so earn the quick nicknames Tall Doctor Dave and Bearded Doctor Dave.

To amuse ourselves during our lengthy van ride to the put-in, we speculate on what the trip might bring. Tall Doctor Dave can do better than speculate, however; he is a Sierra Club member, and the environmentalist group's magazine features an article on the stretch of river we will soon be travelling. He has brought along the article, "Texas on My Mind: Mexico on My Right," and reads us snippets. Author Rebecca Solnit describes our destination as "a slow-moving opaque soup with the occasional clot of foam floating atop it."

In the van, we wince.

In another section, Solnit warns that we will be bobbing through "just about every type of pollution imaginable, including radioactive sediments, industrial toxins, mine wastes, agricultural runoff, erosion caused by mining and logging, and improperly treated sewage."

We wince again, more noticeably this time. Tall Doctor Dave confesses that he almost cancelled the trip and sacrificed his deposit when the magazine arrived in his mailbox, but he really needed a week away from the operating room.

Finally, Solnit writes that the Rio Grande "annually dries up altogether at four points and runs perilously low elsewhere," and details how, because of upstream agricultural diversion, there was barely even enough water for her raft trip to pass through the lower canyons, our destination. She eventually managed to drag her raft out, but leaves the distinct impression that the next party to boat through might get stuck for eternity.

The guides mumble something about Sierra Club negativity, but for the most part the van ride ends in silence.

Saturday afternoon, on the river, paddling like a demon just to keep up with Annie, I see no clots of foam, just lots of cool, quick mud-colored water. The sky is glassy blue, the air sweet smelling, the cliffs gorgeous, and the *Sierra* article is quickly forgotten.

Our first campsite, Borland Canyon, is only five miles off, and with Annie's windmill strokes, we are there in no time. We camp on the Texas side, and at sundown are treated to a light show somewhere south in the Chihuahuan Desert. I have never seen lightning quite like this before; sharp blazing bolts running flat along the horizon, as if the sky itself has been turned on its side.

We finish our evening meal and bed down, then brace for the arrival of the torrential rains that follow the lightning. The storm lasts only ten minutes, but for the duration my tent feels as if it might lift up into the sky.

Morning, though, comes with sunshine, chirping birds, the sound of our lead guide, Fritz, shouting "Cawww-feeeee," in a Southern drawl more like a yodel than a yell. Fritz, a woman despite her nickname, will spend the week keeping us alerted to meals, changes in plans, imminent dangers, and bathroom arrangements. The latter will become quite complicated.

We stumble out of our various tents and take good-natured

inventory of our aches and pains, and our survival. The brief encounter with nature's fury seems to pick up everyone's spirits.

Except Tall Doctor Dave, who emerges sopping wet. His gear is already a running joke — he came on the trip equipped with more rigging than an astronaut, it seems, most of it fluorescent orange or yellow, all of it dramatic on his 6'4" frame. Though we are paddling in extreme heat, he wears enough layered capilene and spandex that he would not look so out of place at a toxic chemical spill. He is a walking advertisement for REI, the catalog outfitter.

Despite his high-tech gear, though, it turns out that he somehow left Chicago without his fly—the taut, waterproof fabric square that stretches over a tent to deflect water away from the edges. As a result, the poor man slept much of the night in a puddle.

As most of us eat breakfast and remark on the beauty of the day, he morosely shoves his drenched equipment and saturated sleeping bag into his gear sack.

"If we can get into camp early," Fritz promises, "and if the sun is still out, and if we can find some trees, that stuff should dry out just fine."

It seems like a lot of ifs, but our first full day on the river is filled with such beauty and interest that even the lanky physician soon forgets to worry.

The immediate riverbank is overwhelmed with bamboo, but the hills on either side host a variety of desert flora—prickly pear cactus, barrel cactus, mesquite, acacia, and ocotillo. The river is a migratory route for birds, since there is extraordinarily little water elsewhere in this desert region, so we see abundant great blue heron, cliff swallows, black phoebes, Swainson hawks. Lu, the birdwatcher, calls out the names for us.

The cliffs, and surrounding bluffs, grow more dramatic with each mile we cover. "Drink," Fritz shouts at regular intervals. "Keep drinking." Confined as we are between canyon walls, under a desert sun, we are baked goods—the real danger to our health and well being, given the gentleness of the rapids so far, is dehydration.

Annie, like the tall doctor, comes well-equipped. She wears a nylon water bag on her back, and drinks constantly from a hose that runs to her mouth. I, on the other hand, come poorly equipped, and am constantly filling, refilling, and dropping my empty Gatorade bottle into the mud on the bottom of the canoe, which always sends us off course, and sends Annie into a short panic.

In this fashion, we put seventeen miles behind us, then camp for our second night on a small, muddy ledge. The canyon walls cut us off from all but the faintest sunlight well before the sun actually sets, and since it is October, we light an early fire. Over a dinner of red beans and rice, we joke about Tall Doctor Dave's wet gear, about which paddling duo is slowest, which the most inept, and which duo bickers most constantly — the two Doctor Daves, it turns out, not Annie and me.

Tall Doctor Dave gives me his copy of the Sierra *article, and that night, in my tent, I underline passages, wondering whether Rebecca Solnit could possibly have been on the same river we now travel.*

Solnit bemoans "longhorn cattle grinding the riverbank into dust" and occasionally washing up dead, "further compromising the river." She mentions possible "killer bees," though she sees none, and "acrid, gritty dust that would blow into every crack in a tent and across every open dish, and onto our exposed skin." Her raft washes aground every few paragraphs, something she blames on all the farmers upstream and their wanton irrigation. At Hot Springs Rapid, our destination for the next evening, she even manages to encounter armed men that she assumes are with the Mexican army.

Solnit, it appears, feels threatened every step of the way; I have never seen such beauty in my life. The few longhorn cattle I see along the riverbank are handsome and welcome. To her, they are uninvited despoilers of the earth. The water on which we paddle is an opaque brown, from the mud, but I am nonetheless grateful for the water, for the heat, for the light dust, for all that I've seen on this first day.

I worried in the van when Tall Doctor Dave started reading the article, worried that the trip brochure promising wild and scenic wilderness was some scam. Now I'm worried about Solnit and her readers and am more than willing to side with the guides and their terse dismissal of predictable "Sierra negativism." I'm not sure what Solnit was looking for on her trip, but I doubt she and I came looking for the same thing.

This unfortunate contradiction in those most committed to environmentalism has been noted before—the very experience of nature, the deep calm and solid centeredness that comes from being in the desert, on the shore, in the forest, is often not available to deeply committed earth activists, because they are perpetually anxious. As stewards of our planetary survival, they sacrifice any opportunity they ever had of enjoying the nature they want to protect.

At one point, Solnit worries in print about the Sierra Blanca nuclear-waste dump. The proposed facility is not even open at the time she is writing (nor is it now), and if it were to open, it would be several hundred miles upstream, and sixteen miles from the river. But, Solnit notes, the proximity of a possible earth-quake fault line "would add to the radioactive threats to the Rio Grande."

If they build it, and if some waste escapes, and if there is an earthquake ... well, it could happen. But I'm thinking, no wonder Solnit's raft kept running aground—she came on her trip carrying a heavy load.

We enter the full force of the canyon on Monday, our third day on the river, and the view becomes truly breathtaking — one-thousand-foot sheer walls, castle-like bluffs, undercut canopies riddled with cliff swallow nests.

Equally striking is the absence of civilization. One other party — a couple in a canoe accompanied by a kayaker — pass by early that morning, but otherwise we seem to be the only humans on the river. Nor is there anyone visible on the adjoining land. The canyon walls make the riverbank, what there is of it, nearly inaccessible for about a seventy-mile stretch; that limits foot-travel, and it limits the canoe and raft traffic as well. Once into the lower canyons, you are in for the duration. It takes a commitment.

During the next few days, we will pass two, maybe three abandoned fishing camps, but see no one, just cows and birds. This remoteness from phones, e-mails, television, and other people, has a wonderfully calming effect. Even the guides eventually relax. We are, Fritz assures us, a "very low maintenance" group of guests.

Tall Doctor Dave encounters a new problem with his size-13 water sandals, but solves it by strapping the sandals onto his feet with duct tape — fluorescent yellow duct tape. Fiona can barely stifle her giggles.

We stop around mid-day at a site the guides promise us is filled with fossils. "You can look at them, but you'll have to leave them where they are," Fritz instructs. A few trip members quote the ecologist's motto, "Leave nothing but your footprints, take nothing but your memories." Gary, one of the guides and a veteran of this canyon, lets us know that he has in fact seen the fossil field dwindle in the ten years or so that he has been making the trip. "They used to be everywhere," he says. "Now you really have to look."

And so we do, baking under the desert sun, turning over countless small sand-colored rocks. We find a few trilobite impressions, one or two fossilized clams, and a living scorpion or two.

We take nothing.

Or if anyone does, no one's telling.

Gradually, we enter deeper into the high canyon, and the river narrows, squeezing more water through an ever-tighter funnel of rock. As a result, the rapids become more potent, more dangerous.

And, as luck would have it, I am the first of the trip to be catapulted out of a boat. A miscalculation of mere inches and I shoot head over heels into Palmas Canyon rapid, a roiling mess of whitewater and rock. My boat, Annie at the bow, carries through the rapid without me. After feeling a blunt impact on my leg, I wash through as well, into a wide, shallow field of riffles and stone.

The guides are quick to throw ropes and shout lifesaving directives that I can't hear over the roar of the water, but none of this turns out to be necessary. Because the temporary widening has created a shallow area, I simply stand up and walk out. I earn a purple bruise the size of a bocce ball on my right thigh but am otherwise unhurt.

My baptism becomes the source of much merriment, and we stop for lunch right where I fell, to mark the occasion. The unpacking of our lunch stores results, however, in a swarm of large, hovering, brown insects known as tarantula hawks.

They are wasps, actually, but very large wasps — roughly the size of small hummingbirds — and are given the striking name because their sting can paralyze a tarantula. The tarantula hawk will drag its immobilized victim away, then deposit its eggs in the body of the living spider. Later, the wasp larva will hatch, and eat their way out.

Gruesome stuff, but they don't sting us. What they desperately want, instead, are our slices of ham. The next twenty minutes consist of swatting and griping, until I distract the group by accidentally discovering a different sort of insect, a rainbow grasshopper. This one is shaped like the grasshopper most of us know, but instead of a dull green or brown, it is covered in bright orange and blue mosaic tiles. It does not seem real; the colors are far too spectacular. But it is. The eyes move cautiously back and forth.

I bring the grasshopper into the group on the twig to which it has attached itself, and everyone crowds around. Solnit never mentioned this.

All of us on the trip have varying levels of experience—with rivers, and with wilderness. The guides, of course, have seen plenty, and many of the paying guests have taken two, even three trips a year for many years running. Often, during our meal breaks, they trade information on destinations and guide companies, thinking ahead to their next excursion.

For me, though, this is a first. I have never experienced so much wilderness in my life, never been so removed from civilization, never been so aware of my own smallness. I would often visit Niagara Falls as a kid, and though there is no denying the majesty of those particular rapids, they somehow weren't as impressive as this canyon. The difference, I decide, must be this: At Niagara Falls, we stand back and observe; here, on this trip, we have become part of the canyon, dependent on the flow of the river, subject to rock and weather, benefiting from the beauty at the same time that we are at risk from the remoteness and harsh geography. We have Igloo coolers, canned ham, bagged rice, and bottled water, so we aren't completely linked to the canyon's ecosystem, but for these seven days, we are beyond doubt at the canyon's mercy. The canyon is mighty

I know perhaps what Solnit would say: The canyon may look pristine, majestic, and intact, but all the while small pollutants we can't see are destroying the delicate natural balance. Just because something looks magnificent, doesn't mean it isn't being destroyed. Look at that footprint, over there! It's not just a footprint, it's erosion.

I appreciate her concern, but even a good thing can be carried too far.

Solnit acknowledges at one point in her article, in fact, that her trip companions, most of them Canadians, seem to be having quite the good time. "But then they were on vacation and determined to enjoy themselves," she writes.

. . .

Wednesday, our fifth day together, the air turns cold, misty, gray, and the paddling grows harder, thanks to a persistent upstream wind. The trip members grow silent; even the guides recede into their thoughts, right down to the vigilant Fritz, who for the first few days would ask "is there anything you need" every twenty minutes.

The weather is surely a factor in our mood, but I think the "canyon effect" becomes part of it as well. None of us feels quite so significant as we did in our civilized other lives. Our verbal cleverness doesn't seem quite so important to share. Who we are, what we own, our job titles — all of these are fairly irrelevant. Our perspective on nature has shifted, but more significantly, so has our perspective on our selves. What we now see, I think, is closer to the truth of the matter.

Only Thomas and Lu remain a team for the full seven days. The rest of us play musical canoes every day or so, switching paddling partners, trying out new seats, new chemistry. Annie paddles now with Gary, one of the guides, and they quickly push out to the lead. Bearded Doctor Dave and I team up, and I'm finally switched to the bow, which affords a nicer view.

This day of dreary weather also brings a series of impassable rapids, or impassable at least in full boats with mid-level paddlers. To get by, we 'line' the boats, which means we stretch out along the rocky bank, brace ourselves against boulders to resist the rushing current, and pull the canoes along one by one, passing them from hand to hand, sometimes hoisting them over rocks too narrow for them to pass through. This is the most dangerous work of the trip. We must take care that the canoes don't come up the line too fast, pinning someone against the rocks, breaking a limb, or worse, forcing one of us underwater where the danger of becoming trapped by the current is great.

After a bit more paddling, we knock off early at a spot called Burro Bluff, one of the highest points within a hundred-mile range. Gunshot thunder is coming from somewhere. Deep as we are in the belly of the canyon, it is hard to tell from exactly where. After our tents are staked and gear stored away, we hike up to the Bluff, past creosote, prickly pear, all manner of thorny plant-life. It is a steep hike — better suited for burros, hence the name, than people — but we are promised a stunning vista.

It takes a good 45 minutes to pull ourselves up the criss-crossing trail, and the view down into the canyon is, indeed, amazing. On a clear day, Fritz tells us, we could see deep into Mexico as well, but the heavy overcast cuts off our view.

We are on the Bluff for no more than two minutes before Fritz realizes the thunder is not so distant, that the storm is close, and bearing right down upon us. "Get your asses down the hill," she shouts, not needing to explain. We are standing on the highest point anywhere near, human lightning rods.

The run back down is a comic stumble, the small rocks catching under foot like ball-bearings, the cacti snagging and scratching, the wonderful view forgotten. The canyon rules all.

I do love the planet, though if Solnit were reading this essay as closely as I've read hers, I suspect she would not think so. I am firmly against acid runoff, nuclear spillage, diverted rivers, and a host of other ecological evils. I believe that we all would do better to cooperate with the Earth's ecosystem rather than run it into the ground. I think myself a reasonable man. But Solnit might lump me in with the irrigators, the lumber harvesters, the cattlemen, and all the others guilty of insensitive exploitation.

After all, I'm only human.

Of course, in some environmentalist writing, that's precisely the problem: the human species is the only thing separating a contaminated planet from Eden. If the "cancer" we call human beings were to be cut away, some seem to imply, then all our problems would somehow be solved. Whatever we do, however we interact with the environment is unnatural; whatever every other species does is as natural as rain. On this trip, we are hauling out not just our garbage and food waste, but our human waste as well, in that big tin box called the Groaner. Yet cows and goats and pigs and birds have been defecating along this river forever. They didn't seem to ruin anything. Tarantula hawks lay their eggs inside of live scorpions, so that their offspring can hatch and eat their way out, but that's natural. We, on the other hand, have to apologize for paddling up to the shoreline with our little tents, because we are flattening some grass, and maybe leaving a footprint or two.

What seems most pointless to me is the either/or nature of the argument. The Bible tells us that mankind has "dominion over the fish of the sea, and over the fowl of the air, and over the cattle, and over all the earth," and some interpret this to mean we can do as we please, when we please, without thought or moral center. The ecological extremists, on the other hand, seem to see us as the only species not entitled to interact with the Earth at all.

I don't see much of a future in either position.

Annie has made it clear to us that she shares some of Solnit's views, but with an added gender twist. "Back before the sky gods came, before history," she tells us during one of our snack breaks, "the earth was a matriarchy. There was no question where the power was – women were the ones who gave birth, so they had all the authority. Men had no idea if they even played a part in the birth process, so they had no sense of their own importance.

"But then women put men in charge of metallurgy, and everything changed," she explains. "That's why we're destroying the planet. The patriarchy is only concerned with maximum production. Men have no interest in nurturing, in preserving anything. All the patriarchy wants to do is produce more, more, more."

I am more than a little chagrined, then, when it is Annie who later catches me in an act of environmental misconduct.

So far we have camped on slabs of rock, on mud, on sand, once even on grass, but our Thursday evening campsite is a field of small stones. My ten-year-old daughter, Maria, collects stones, and when I wake up Friday, I can't resist the urge to gather a few of the more uniquely colored or patterned ones to bring her as my return gift. I am aware that this violates the strict "take nothing but your memories" rule, but my love for my daughter overtakes my conscience.

Annie, though, comes upon me as I collect a plastic baggie of pebbles. We are in a rock sea, billions of rocks washed down from the cliffs and unearthed by the river over thousands, maybe millions of years, but Annie catches on quickly to what I am doing, narrows her eyes.

Futilely, I try to convince her of my position. "A few rocks aren't going to make a difference," I say, pointing to the small stones all around.

That doesn't seem to impress her, so I lamely play a gender card, "They're for my daughter."

"You shouldn't take a thing," Annie answers with a chill. "Nothing."

This is the official position of the trip guides as well, but Fritz and her crew have no interest in policing our gear. Thomas and Lu, in fact, have for the last day or so been lifting rocks the size of footballs into their canoe. They are building a fireplace back home and explain to me that they like to use rocks from each of their many adventure travel trips as architectural accents. Fritz says, "You really shouldn't do that" at one point, but otherwise lets the infraction slide. I don't know if Annie has said anything to them or not.

Later, Bearded Doctor Dave shares his own views of nature.

"Oh, these environmentalists are worrying for no reason," he says cheerfully. "We aren't going to destroy the planet. Nature always takes care of herself. When we get too many people around here, when things get too bad, nature will intervene."

"How?" I ask.

"Plague," he answers dispassionately. "It is only a matter of time before the planet is hit with its next widescale de-population. There are viruses out there we don't know about yet. Nature cleans its own house."

He is a physician, so we listen closely.

Moments later, Lu, reflecting on the imminent end of our trip, says, "My, we have been out of touch for so long. There are people out there wondering if we are still alive."

"We should be wondering if they are still alive," Bearded Doctor Dave answers quickly. "It's more dangerous in their world with all the car accidents, shootings, muggings, bombings, than it is out here. Why do you even assume at this point that your loved ones back home are still alive?"

We paddle the rest of the day with little said between us.

It has come down to this:

Rebecca Solnit seems convinced that we are marring the planet willfully and with malice. Bearded Doctor Dave, it turns out, shares her views in his own odd way, but is instead focused on the ecosystem's coming revenge, the quiet shy planet striking back with a fury. Annie agrees with Solnit, and in addition, is fairly sure I'm one of the worst offenders. Thomas and Lu are collecting stones for their fireplace and taking it all in stride. We are, all of us on the trip, dirty, tired, cold, scratched and bruised, and as best as I can tell, the river is doing just fine. No one has seen a single clot of toxic foam.

We have met nature, debated our place in it, and found little common ground.

As for me, I don't object to using a big tin box for a toilet, and I even take my turn carrying the heavy receptacle on and off the canoe each day; and I don't mind carrying away all of our trash, right down to straining out the few grains of rice that fall into our dishwater when we do the pots and pans; I even follow the rule to bag up my apple cores, though I still contend the wildlife would have been more grateful had we left them. I don't mind any of it, really, but I object to the implication that we somehow don't belong, that our every step is unnatural and unwelcome.

As careful as we are, the fact remains that at each of our seven campsites we have squashed some bugs, flattened some plants, inadvertently knocked the needles off a few cacti, and eroded a bit of soil off the muddy banks as we scrambled up with our considerable gear. Do I have to feel horrible about this?

A friend of mine, an Appalachian hiker, has explained to me that anti-environmentalists are guilty of exaggerating the environmentalist position, that the entire environmental movement is being tarred with an eco-extremist brush to make the environmentalists' views easier to dismiss.

This is an old tactic, and I'm sure he is right. I don't mean to contribute to this distortion, but I have Solnit's article in front of me. And Annie really said those things. And I gave those rocks to my daughter, and still feel vaguely uneasy about whether I did the right or wrong thing.

My behavior has not been blameless, maybe, but it hasn't been so bad. Yes, I believe in the beauty and importance of the environment, and I believe in protecting it. But I'd also like to be a part of it. Call it selfish if you will, but I'd be quicker to support the preservation of an ecosystem that includes me as a regular member.

I didn't visit the river in a bulldozer, after all.

I came by canoe.

Reprinted from: *Arts & Letters: Journal of Contemporary Culture* (Issue Two, Fall 1999)

About the Authors

Britt Allen is an award-winning poet who graduated with her Master of Arts degree in Literature and Writing from Utah State University in May 2020, where she now teaches academic writing. She is interested in the eroticism of violence in female confessional and lyric poetry, contributing her own experiences and voice with her art. She lives in northern Utah with her partner and rescue dog. Her first chapbook, *Harvest,* is being published summer 2021 by Finishing Line Press. Follow her work at brittallen.org.

Living nestled within the peaks of Northern Utah, **Betti Avari** spends her days absorbed in story and her sleepless nights tucked under a fuzzy blanket, typing her truth—or latest nightmare. Writing is her coping mechanism. She admits that she doesn't seek to add nightmares to this life, only a way through those that already exist, and she writes because life is too short not to.

Marilyn Ball is an award-winning poet whose work celebrates the awe-inspiring grandeur, soul-stirring connection to, and restorative power of the outdoors. Marilyn is a long time member of the Heritage Writers Guild and the Utah State Poetry Society. She is a crowd favorite at poetry readings, and her work routinely takes top honors in creative writing contests.

Her work has appeared in numerous journals, collections, and anthologies, including *In the Shimmering, Volatile When Mixed,* and *Sand and Sky: poems from Utah.*

Shanan Ballam is the Poet Laureate for Logan City, Utah. She is the author of the poetry chapbook *The Red Riding Hood Papers* and two full-length poetry collections *Pretty Marrow* and *Inside the Animal: The Collected Red Riding Hood Poems.* She earned an MFA in poetry writing from the University of Nebraska, Omaha, studying under her mentor, William Trowbridge, former Poet Laureate of Missouri. She teaches poetry writing and composition for Utah State University and was selected as the 2014 Lecturer of the Year for the College of Humanities & Social Sciences. She served on the Utah Arts Council Board of Directors as the Literary Arts Representative from 2013-2017.

Jeff Bateman served in the U.S. Air Force for 32 years, retiring as a colonel in 2010. He teaches courses in American history at Utah State University. Jeff is the author of *On the Death Beat,* and co-author of *No Peace with the Dawn,* with E.B. Wheeler. He lives in North Central Arizona, where horses, gardening, and playing the bass in a rock band fill the time he isn't writing or teaching.

Alice M. Batzel is a published author, playwright, journalist, and poet. A displaced beach writer from the northwest Florida gulf coast, Alice is an advocate for literacy through lifelong reading and writing. Her current writing projects include humor stories, a middle-grade detective mystery, a female detective novel for adults and young adults, a romantic comedy novel, and a collection of Christmas stories.

Alice and her husband reside in a rural community at the foot of the majestic Wasatch mountains of northern Utah. Readers can follow Alice on her websitewww.alicembatzel.com and through social media on her Facebook author page https://www.facebook.com/people/Author-Alice-M-Batzel/100034795072248

Eric Bishop is a dad to four, husband to one, and grandpa to three. His debut novel, *The Samaritan's Pistol*, was called, "Taut, refreshing and well-paced" by Publisher's Weekly. Long on imagination but short on writing skills, he credits the Cache Valley chapter of the League of Utah Writers for helping him learn everything needed to get published.

Star Coulbrooke is the Inaugural Poet Laureate of Logan City, Utah and co-founder of the Helicon West Reading Series. Her most recent poetry collections are *Thin Spines of Memory, Both Sides from the Middle,* and *City of Poetry.*

Brock Dethier retired in 2018 after teaching at Utah State University for 21 years and directing the composition program since 2007. He has published five books for college composition teachers and students as well as two volumes of poetry. His song-and-story albums for kids are available at Amazon.com and Bandcamp.com.

In 2006 and 2012, he was chosen as the teacher of the year for the College of Humanities and Social Sciences. He serves as a judge for the USU creative writing contest every year.

Dustin Earl earned a bachelor's degree in history from Utah State University. He spent several years teaching English in China but has recently returned home to Utah. His writing is featured in several anthologies, including *Volatile When Mixed* and *Intersections.*

Matthew Funk was born and raised in Northern Utah. He lives on the family farm with his wife and four daughters. His work has also appeared in *Chasing Tomorrow.*

Lorin Grace was born in Colorado and has been moving around the country ever since, living in eight states and several imaginary worlds. She holds a degree in graphic design, which comes in handy with creating book covers. Currently, she lives with her husband and a dog who is insanely jealous of her laptop. When not writing, Lorin enjoys creating graphics, visiting historical sites, museums, painting furniture, and reading. Three of her books, her debut novel, *Waking Lucy* (2017), *Mending Fences* (2018), and *Not the Bodyguard's Baby* (2020), have won Recommend Read awards in the League of Utah Writers' Quills Awards.

Jo Lynne Harline is a seasoned hiker, backpacker, camper, girls' camp leader, river runner, and earth steward. She and her husband took their kids on many outdoor adventures as they grew up. She is a writer, a member of both Utah Statewide Archaeological Society and League of Utah Writers.

Jef Huntsman is the highly acclaimed and award-winning published author of five fiction and two non-fiction books, numerous short stories, and delightful poetry. He was voted Utah's Writer of the Year in 2017 for his Carson series thriller, *Jamaica Rush,* and his dedicated service to the literary community. He spends most of his time writing from his loft, swimming, hiking, or enjoying the peace of raging flames from his under-the-stars firepit at his cabin in central Utah.

Jefhuntsmanauthor.com

McKel Jensen wants to discover the origin of language. To facilitate her curiosity, she keeps uncovering clues as she puts words together on the page. Having grown up in the shadow of Mt. Olympus in the Salt Lake Valley, McKel learned to respect the simplicity and majesty of nature. She later studied literature of the outdoors as she worked toward her BA from Utah State University and MA from Weber State University. Although she may not know the meaning of all things—yet—she is living life as fully as she can while raising three young kids with her husband in Brigham City. She also wants it to be clear that although her friendship with Laurel was real, her friend is very much alive and raising five beautiful daughters in North Carolina.

Tim Keller is an avid reader who also has a weak spot for monster movies. He likes traveling, 80's music, and if the highway patrol is to be believed, driving way too fast. After working as a bouncer, mortgage researcher, computer repair technician, caregiver, and a brief, albeit disastrous, stint as a waiter in anachronistic drag, he decided he wanted to be a writer when he grew up. A keen observer of human nature, Tim enjoys writing stories about all kinds of people from all walks of life. His work can be found in various literary journals and anthologies including *Mirrored Realities, In the Shimmering, Between Places, The Helicon West Anthology, The Unraveling,* and *Joyride.*

Dinty W. Moore is author of the memoirs *Between Panic & Desire*, and *To Hell With It*, the writing guides *The Story Cure, Crafting the Personal Essay*, and *The Mindful Writer*, among other books. He has published essays and stories in *Harper's, The New York Times Magazine, The Southern Review, The Georgia Review, Kenyon Review, Creative Nonfiction*, and elsewhere.

Stephen Page is part Native American and part Scottish. He was born in Detroit. He is the author of four books of poetry - "The Salty River Bleeds," "A Ranch Bordering the Salty River," "The Timbre of Sand," and "Still Dandelions." He holds two AA's from Palomar College, a BA from Columbia University, and an MFA from Bennington College. He also attended Broward College. His literary criticisms have appeared regularly in the Buenos Aires Herald, How Journal, Gently Read Literature, North of Oxford, and the Fox Chase Review. His stories have been published in Amphibi, Birch Book Press, Bold + Italic, October Hill, Quarto, and The Whistling Fire. He is the recipient of a First Place Prize in Poetry from Bravura, the Jess Cloud Memorial Prize, a Writer-in-Residence from the Montana Artists Refuge, a Full Fellowship from the Vermont-Studio Center, an Imagination Grant from Cleveland State University, and an Arvon Foundation Ltd. Grant. He loves his wife, family, friends, nature, long walks through woodlands, solitude, journaling, spontaneous road trips, riding motorcycles, throwing cellphones into lakes, dog-earring pages in books, and making noise on his electric bass.

Felicia Rose has published in The Westchester Review, The Dandelion Review, Mother Earth News, The Way to My Heart: An Anthology of Food-Related Romance, The Sun, The

Change Agent: An Adult Education Magazine for Social Justice, The Lavender Review, and elsewhere. A New York City native, she is now returning home after eight years in Cache Valley, Utah.

Jennifer Sinor is the author of several books of literary nonfiction, most recently *Sky Songs: Meditations on Loving a Broken World* (University of Nebraska Press). Her other books include *Letters Like the Day: On Reading Georgia O'Keeffe* (University of New Mexico Press) and the memoir *Ordinary Trauma* (University of Utah Press). The recipient of the Stipend in American Modernism as well as nominations for the National Magazine Award and the Pushcart Prize, Jennifer teaches creative writing at Utah State University where she is a professor of English.

Isaac Timm was born and raised in the western desert town of Callao, Utah, a stop on the historic Pony Express trail. His highest aspiration is to be a storyteller like his father. He is a graduate of Utah State University in history and English. His poetry and short stories have won numerous awards.

Chadd VanZanten writes narrative nonfiction essays and literary short stories, no one of which is really much truer than any of the others. His fiction has been published in numerous anthologies, including *Creep Factor: Thirteen Deeply Creepy Horror Stories* (Knowledge Forest Press 2018), and in his short story collection *The Key To This Whole Entire Thing* (Knowledge Forest Press 2019). He is also the author of works on fly-fishing and backpacking, including *On Fly-Fishing The Wind Rivers* (The History Press 2018).

E.B. Wheeler earned graduate degrees in history and in landscape architecture from Utah State University. She is the award-winning author of twelve books for children and adults, including *The Bone Map, No Peace with the Dawn, Blood in a Dry Town,* and Whitney Award finalist *Born to Treason,* as well as several short stories, magazine articles, and scripts for educational software programs. In the summer, she is often working in her garden or exploring the Intermountain West. You can find more about her books at https://www. amazon.com/E.B.-Wheeler/e/B00VKQG6MO or ebwheeler.com

www.ingramcontent.com/pod-product-compliance
Lightning Source LLC
Chambersburg PA
CBHW071622030726
47598CB00001B/391